EXPRESS EXEC

EXPRESS EXEC

A Novel Approach to Outrunning the Pace of Change

Gary Brose

CC Productions
4005 20th Ave West #133
Seattle, WA 98199

Edition #1

ISBN: 9781642372236

Published by CC Productions 07/15/18

Other books by Gary Brose:

Bonus Your Way to Profits
The Ultimate Motivated Employee
How to Get a Raise

A PREFACE FROM THE AUTHOR

This may end up being the most unusual business book you've ever read. I tried multiple times to write this as I normally would—you know, identify a problem facing business people, give some real-life examples, and then start in on instructions. I planned to cover it in five easy steps, and then as I outlined those, it became nine easy steps, then thirteen, then I realized it would be over fifteen steps and none of them were easy. So I bailed.

I went back to the drawing board and rethought the entire concept. I wanted the reader to feel the real-world pain, fear, angst, and joy too, just as you would in real life if you were trying to lead a department or company through massive change. Finally, after discussing it with a friend and sharing how much I enjoyed writing novels rather than business books, he suggested I do just that. After laughing it off, I realized writing the book in novel form, telling a story, would give me the opportunity to immerse the reader in the trials and tribulations of the protagonist.

So, I started writing and *Express Exec* is the final product. My goal is to help business owners and managers learn the keys to building a foundation that will allow you to make change happen rapidly without totally alienating your workforce. And, in fact, helping those employees to also come to grips with doing battle against the pace of change. That, dear reader, is a never-ending battle, and if you haven't faced it yet, I assure you, it's coming around the bend at you at full speed!

MONDAY, JANUARY 22

It was Monday, January 22nd—the day that her whole world changed. Andrea Lane checked her watch, rose from her desk, and quietly closed her office door.

I have just enough time to finish Charlie Jensen's performance review. It's not going to be a good one, but he deserves to know the truth, she thought.

She returned to her desk and began pounding on the keyboard. Writing always came easy to Andrea. From her first days in school to her first job, she found she could write brief, coherent memos and letters far faster than any of her coworkers.

Gotta go with your strengths. That's what Uncle Tyler always says.

She continued typing, filling out the form and including examples of what Charlie had done or failed to do as supervisor of Lines 3 and 4. As she reached the end, she hesitated. Checking her watch again, she realized she had less than three minutes to wrap it up.

What can I say here that won't sound too harsh but will still make him realize he has to shape up now, not later?

Suddenly, filled with inspiration, she typed the last sentence.

Charlie, you are a good person with good intentions, but your work product needs to improve and quickly. I'm fearful that without improvement in Line 3's and 4's productivity, your future at Juggernaut Enterprises could be in jeopardy.

She printed out two copies and signed her name to both. Time was up. She smiled to herself as she headed down the hall toward Mr. Bentley's hastily scheduled meeting at four o'clock.

Arthur Bentley hated to be kept waiting. When a manager was late to a meeting, he would hand the offender a stopwatch and make a note of who was holding it now. That person got every unwanted job that came up until the next meeting came around and it was handed off to the next late person.

This meeting was called with practically no notice, and Mr. Bentley's meager patience was already stretched thin. His somber look gave everyone a preview about today's contents. Andrea walked into the conference room ten seconds after four o'clock. Her tardiness earned her a steely-eyed stare from the CEO.

She sat down as Mr. Bentley walked over to Robbie Carter, the VP of Logistics, and relieved him of the dreaded stopwatch he held. Robbie couldn't contain himself, flashing a brief grin of relief and joy. He tried to erase it quickly as he glanced at Andrea and saw Bentley's presentation of the watch into her waiting palm.

"Ms. Lane, you were late. You'll be getting every shit job that comes up from now on."

Andrea did her best to smile at the news but wasn't quite able to pull it off.

The CEO hastened back up front and said, "I'm going to get right to it. It's no secret that our costs have risen and profit margin has dropped precipitously in the last year." He paused and, looking at Robbie, said, "You do know what precipitously means, don't you, Mr. Carter?" Robbie, the only VP at Juggernaut without a college education, was Bentley's favorite target when he wanted to belittle someone.

"Um, yes, it means downward, uh, swiftly," Robbie replied.

His fun ruined, Bentley continued, "I had a long meeting with the bankers yesterday. They have declined to extend our line of credit by another six million dollars, which we need to purchase the Glimmer Stones and other products needed for our next round of production."

Every one of the five VPs exchanged worried glances.

At the opposite end of the table from Bentley was seated the VP of Operations, Craig Saunders. On the left side of the conference table were Gretchen Hubbard, the VP of Marketing, and Tim Russell, the VP of Finance. Robbie Carter, the VP of Logistics, joined Andrea on the right. Sammi Wright, the VP of Human Resources, was away on vacation.

"Don't you go worrying. We can take it out of savings and slow down payment cycles to cover this bill, but it's the next one we won't be able to cover if the bank doesn't change their mind. The bank said they would review our financials again in early July, giving us nearly six months to, you know, spruce up a bit."

Cluelessly, Gretchen raised her hand and interrupted Bentley. "Sir, we can't make the Value Vases without the Glimmer Stones. What will we do if they don't change their minds?"

The look Bentley gave Gretchen would have caused a heart attack in someone more in tune with the moment, but Gretchen simply stared back at him.

"That's the crux of the problem, dammit!" Bentley roared, his loud voice belying his diminutive stature. Sweeping his right hand across the room, he continued, "And it's all because you people aren't working hard enough. We need to cut costs and increase sales. Now!" He stopped to take a sip of his water and down another aspirin.

Then he launched into it again. "So listen up. The bank has given us time to turn the company around. Six months to stop the bleeding. Six months to increase sales. *Or else!* And if they don't finance us, no one will. You get it? We're over. We're done. I'll have to close the doors. Now, not a word of this to the rank-and-file employees. This is top secret. Don't even tell your wives or husbands. I want a plan on my desk by eight a.m. on Friday. A plan from every one of you to turn your department around. And it better be good or I'll bounce you out so fast your head will spin. Got it?"

Bentley stormed out of the room as though he couldn't stand their presence any longer.

After he left, everyone stayed seated as if they were glued to their chair. Silence reigned until Craig rose from his seat, ran a hand through his wavy salt-and-pepper hair, snapped his briefcase closed, and left without a word. A mass exodus followed him.

Arriving home that evening, Andrea entered her apartment and immediately had a terrible thought.

If I lose this job, I'll have to live off my savings. There goes all the effort I've made over the last four years to save every spare nickel for the condo down payment. I'll have to stay here in this dark apartment for a lot longer. Oh, God, I'm so screwed...

Andrea tied her pitch-black hair into a ponytail, popped a TV dinner into the microwave, and poured a glass of mineral water. Then, thinking better of it, she opened the bottle of wine she was saving for the weekend and poured a generous glassful. "Not much point in saving it now," she said to herself.

She sat down at her kitchen nook table and took a few bites of her chicken and almonds TV dinner. She downed some chardonnay and realized she didn't actually have an appetite. Walking away from the table, she took her glass of wine and stretched out on her corduroy couch.

I think I'll just lay here. This is crazy. What can I do? I'm just the Interim VP of Manufacturing. I'm only in this spot because Howard Fuller quit three months ago and Bentley stuck me in his role. What I do can't impact the whole company. Well, whatever. I'm just going to lie down and have a pity party the size of Texas.

The next day, she checked her stats report showing manufacturing's production from last week. Again production was low and she wandered onto the floor to visit with Charlie Jensen, her lead Supervisor.

Charlie wasn't around, but she spotted his number two man, Sheldon Rogers.

"Shell, I see we must have had some problems last week. Production was down thirty-five percent."

Without even looking at Andrea, he said, "The usual. You know, Line 3 went down at 1:15 and we were out of the two-inch ball bearings needed to fix it. So we ordered some more and they got here yesterday. We're back up now."

"When did this happen?"

"Um, I guess it was last Friday night," Sheldon said.

Andrea looked at him as her eyes grew wide. "We lost a day and a half due to not having the supplies we needed?"

"Well, no, um, it was closer to a day and a quarter. And we didn't really *lose* the days. We still operated by moving everyone to Line 4. It was way slower, but we still got things done, sort of. Something was going on with all the VPs, so we didn't want to bother you with it. It got fixed."

Seeing Sheldon's lack of concern about productivity, Andrea lost the will to fight it and went back to her office. Sitting down at her desk, she placed her head in her hands and fought off the urge to panic.

I'm up against it now. How am I going to make big changes when no one else gives a damn? I've got to—

"Andrea, got a minute?"

Robbie Carter, all six-foot-three of him, stood in the doorway with a hopeful look on his face.

"Sure, come on in. What's up, Robbie?"

"So, just, you know, wonderin'. You got any great ideas yet? I mean, to give to Bentley on Friday?"

Andrea took a deep breath and released it slowly. "I've been giving him and Howard ideas of what I could do for three years now and they never liked any of them. I'm starting to think the best idea is to polish up my resume."

"Funny," Robbie said, "I was thinkin' the same thing. But then I looked at my crew and thought about how many of them have families to support and people counting on that paycheck and, well, running away seems sort of like a selfish option."

Andrea said nothing for the longest time. Finally, she got up and said, "I'm going home. I don't feel well. Maybe I'll get an idea or two if I rest for a bit."

With that, she headed out the door.

TUESDAY, JANUARY 23

ndrea didn't go home. She walked the streets of her neighborhood and searched her mind for some answers. Usually when she walked, new thoughts and exciting plans would attack her from all sides. She'd ask herself, *Why can't we do something different?* And then after mulling it over for a while, an idea would present itself to her and she would get this odd feeling of excitement in her stomach. She'd hustle home and sit at the nook table and write down bullet points outlining her new idea. The rest of that day and night she would feel like she was floating; like anything was possible. That led to more dreams of promotions and making more money and buying that perfect condo…and even more excited feelings.

Today, no such ideas came to her. She ended her walk and headed home.

As she crossed Delano Street, she looked a few blocks down and could see the lighted sign of Tyler's place, the aptly named Professor's Bar and Grill. She turned and headed that way.

Walking into Uncle Tyler's place at three in the afternoon on a workday was certainly something she'd never done before.

Tyler took one look at her and instantly knew she was in a bad way.

"Andi, what are you doing here?"

Trying her best to keep it light, she replied, "Slumming. Wanted to see how the famous Professor's Bar and Grill was doing on a weekday."

Tyler, a balding, sixty-three-year-old, ex-professor, said, "Hey, slumming is *my* job. And as you can see"—he swept his arm in the air, pointing from one end of the building to the other—"this is not the busiest time of the day. Give me an hour or two and I'll impress you with how busy I am."

Andrea forced herself to return the obligatory chuckle and took a seat at the bar.

"The usual?" Tyler asked.

"You mean you're stocked up on Shirley Temples?"

"Just for you!"

"Not this time, Unc. I think I need something stronger."

Tyler returned with a glass of Merlot and parked himself across the bar from his niece. Tyler had been a Professor of Economics for twenty years at State U, but one day he shucked it all and walked away. He wanted to do something completely different. He was a voracious reader and a student of human nature and he wanted to study people in real life, not in theory. So he opened a bar and worked when he felt like it. When he did work, he talked to everyone who came in and later made notes about what he'd learned. He turned those notes into two books, both published by major publishing houses, and now he lived off his pension, profits from the bar, and his considerable book royalties.

Andrea stared at her uncle and did her best to keep a stiff upper lip. She had never been a frail flower, but this latest turn of events had shaken her to the core. The one constant in her life after her parents died young had been Uncle Tyler. His IQ was off the charts, he was successful on multiple levels, and Andrea trusted him completely. He'd always been the one to turn to when she had to think out a critical decision.

"So," Tyler said slowly. "You going to tell me what's up?"

"Why does something have to be up?" she countered.

Tyler rolled his eyes and said, "Maybe because it's written all over your face?"

She hesitated, then said, "I'll tell you, but you can't tell anybody else." She stretched out her words as though each syllable was painful.

7

"Somebody's giving you grief because you're half Korean, right?" Tyler asked, tensing up.

"No," Andrea said, "nothing like that."

Tyler relaxed back into his chair and waited for her to continue when she was ready.

The bar's lone customer finished his beer and left. They both watched him exit.

Satisfied she had stalled as long as she could, she said, "Juggernaut is in big financial trouble. I'm going to lose my job within six months."

Tyler let out a sigh of relief. "Oh, jeez, Andi, I thought maybe it was some love interest who'd done you wrong. I was getting ready to introduce him to Tyler's Special Aluminum Knee-breaking Bat."

That got Andrea to break into a smile. This time she gave a real chuckle.

"No, I haven't had time for boyfriends lately. And the ones I did have time for all turned out to be the same—macho men, conceited, and unconcerned about anyone besides themselves. The problem is Bentley. And the way we do things at Juggernaut." She proceeded to tell him all about the meeting, mixing in multiple admonishments against disclosure of any of the information. She told him more than she had ever shared with him before about her job and the company and the lack of urgency that permeates the business. She told him how she felt powerless to change anything. When she was finished, she tapped her empty glass and eyed him.

"So, your response is to drink yourself into oblivion?" Tyler asked, only half-kidding.

"Two glasses of wine is hardly oblivion. Unc, I've spent seven years of my life trying to learn this business and move up, and now what? I wasted all those years?" Andrea replied.

Tyler poured her another glass and told her he was cutting her off.

Andrea smiled and nodded, knowing her protective uncle always worried about her.

After a couple minutes of silence, Tyler said, "Well, realistically, there is nothing you can do to change the inevitable. I guess you're just screwed. Nothing you can do about it. It just is. No point in trying now to make a difference."

Feeling hurt that he was giving up on her so fast, Andrea retorted, "Well, I-I thought you might have better advice for me than that."

"Why bother?" Tyler said. "Looks to me like you're already throwing in the towel."

Tyler walked away and began moving dirty glasses into the dishwasher. When he finished, he went out of sight into the back room and returned a few minutes later with a stack of bills that needed paying.

Andrea took another sip of her wine, placed a ten-dollar bill next to it, and got off the bar stool. She put her jacket on and mumbled a good-bye. Tyler didn't look up. He just muttered his good-bye too. She exited the bar and headed back up Delano Street toward her apartment.

Six minutes later, she re-entered the still-empty bar and, before the door had slammed shut behind her, called out, "I never said I was giving up! I've got ideas. I could still make a difference!"

Tyler looked at her with a huge smile pasted on his face. "Well, what took you so long? Ever since you were a little girl, you never took any crap. You always stood up to fight. I thought maybe you lost that little girl, but now I see she's back."

"Damn right I'm back. I just got knocked down a bit, that's all. I can get back up again. I don't want to lose this job, Unc. Help me! Help me figure out what I can do."

"Sit down on your stool and I'll get you some ice water." He delivered the water to her and asked, "You said you'd submitted a slew of ideas up the ladder and he never agreed to any of them, right?"

"That's true. Bentley always said they'd cost too much, or they'd upset the other managers, or he was concerned about set- ting a bad precedent. He had a million excuses," Andrea recounted, words flowing quickly now.

"Maybe they were bad ideas," Tyler tried.

"No! No, they were good. They're still good. He's just old-fashioned. He keeps saying the way we've always done it is good enough. It's change he doesn't want. At least that's what I think."

"If your ideas are good, then resubmit them."

"He'll just say no again," Andrea lamented.

Tyler just stared at her.

She stared back.

Suddenly, she knew why he wasn't talking. "Oh, I know. I know. You always say it and I always forget it. The man—or woman…you know, it *could* be a woman, so let me rephrase it for you. The woman who takes no for an answer didn't ask enough questions."

"That's right," Tyler agreed, grinning. "You go back in there and fight for your ideas. Andrea, you are best when you fight for the things you believe in. You fight until he says yes. You tell him he's facing the end of the company in six months. And if he doesn't pull out all the stops, if he doesn't try everything and anything, then he's doomed. You ask him, 'If not now, when?'"

"Yes! You're right! What does he have to lose?"

"That's the Andrea I know!" He gazed at his niece, pride in his eyes, a smile on his face. His wheels were turning too. "You know, Andrea, part of the problem is you're too close to it. You're thinking about business *inside* your company. I'm telling you, I can't solve those problems for you; *you* have to do it yourself. All I can do is point you in the right direction, and I'm telling you, you have to look beyond the company to the whole world outside it."

Andrea cocked her head and asked, "What do you mean?"

"I mean while Juggernaut has stood still, doing the same things it always has, the world has changed. And more importantly, the pace of change has increased exponentially. This world is full of companies like Juggernaut that aren't adjusting, aren't changing along with it. And all those companies are going to find themselves passed by—by a world that is careening down a path far different from what they are on."

Feeling some of that odd excitement in her gut again, Andrea willed him on. "I'm listening."

Tyler was truly in his element—teaching once again. "Andrea, everything is different now. And if something *isn't* different, it soon will be. Look around you. Look at people's shoes. Fifty years ago, if you got a hole in your sole, you took your shoes to a shoemaker and he repaired it for you. Why? Because the price of a pair of shoes was a higher percentage of monthly income than it is now. Now, relative prices are lower and income is higher. People just throw their shoes out and buy new ones. Every product has a shorter life span. People are used to buying a cell phone and replacing it one or two years later. Did it break? No. They just choose to because they can, because the new models have more features or they wanted to be more stylish or popular or whatever."

Tyler was on fire now. He walked around the bar and waved his hands every which way as he spoke ever more quickly. "Every day more apps, devices, software, inventions, everything is being created for the masses. Juggernaut sells expensive vases, patio furniture, rugs, and dozens of other household products that are the same today as they were fifty years ago. Back then, people valued quality goods. Now, in most cases, quality is relative and instant gratification is the trend. Everybody wants it now, so rapid distribution is king. Quality is not as important anymore. You need to look at trends and styles, fads and changing habits, and all the things that govern a person's life and ask yourself, 'How does my company fit in? How do we meet their new needs?' And then you have to build an organization that is focused not on its own product, but on the people who buy it. Your job isn't to please Bentley. Your job is to please the buyers."

He paused briefly, then finished his thought. "You see, in order to keep up with the world, you have to escalate the pace with which you do everything. You have to look at everything your company is doing and find ways to speed it up. Every function—manufacturing, sales, data collection, marketing, A/R collections, hiring, everything—has to be done faster and smarter."

Almost out of breath, Tyler leaned back and relaxed for a moment.

Andrea stared at him, and a slow smile appeared on her face. "It's a lot to do, but…" Her voice trailed off as her mind started conjuring up a game plan.

"I haven't told you the toughest part yet," Tyler said, as he walked back behind the bar.

A moment of true fear crossed her face as Andrea asked, "What's the toughest part?"

Tyler poured himself a shot of Bourbon and downed it in one swallow.

"It can't just be *you*. You have to build systems that run almost on autopilot, systems that measure everything about your market, your buyers, and your productivity. And with the pace of change increasing exponentially, you have to constantly stay on top of it, maybe even get ahead of the curve, and continue to evolve. And the day your business stops evolving, that's the day it starts to die."

SATURDAY, JANUARY 27

Delano Street was quiet that Saturday morning as Andrea headed to Uncle Tyler's bar for an early morning meeting. She knocked on the window next to the door and peered in. Tyler nodded and unlocked the front door, greeting her with a hug.

"I'm glad you're here. I can't wait to hear about all you've done."

Andrea looked around the empty room, then pointed to herself. "Are you talking to me? The woman who hasn't done anything yet?"

"Sit down and tell me about it. I have coffee brewing and I picked up one of those big blueberry muffins from the bakery for you."

Andrea perked up. "I love those!"

"I know. That's why I bought it."

"You didn't have to. Very thoughtful, Unc. I can't remember the last time someone did something special just for me."

Tyler smiled. "I thought I'd start off the meeting with a good business lesson."

Andrea eyed him. "What do you mean?"

"We'll come back to that later," Tyler said. He finished pouring the coffee and returned the pot to the burner. Setting a manila folder on the table, he sat down and said, "Tell me about your week."

Andrea filled him in on the last few days. She told him about her meeting with Bentley and how he shot down every idea she had. Again. She told Tyler about meeting with all the other VPs for drinks on Thursday night and how devoid of any real action plans they were.

"Nothing?" Tyler asked. "They had no ideas at all?"

"I didn't mean that," Andrea lamented. "But all the ideas they had were, you know, business as usual stuff. Cut costs, lay off a few people. Add a sales rep. Get everyone to work faster and harder. That kind of stuff."

Tyler took a sip of his coffee and said, "Tell me about these folks. Who are they? Give me a one sentence description that sums them up."

Andrea rolled her eyes. "OK, let me think. One sentence. All right, here we go. Craig Sanders is the top ranked VP. He should be CEO but Bentley won't give that title up, so he's called the VP of Ops and is supposed to be in charge of everything. He's old-school, and his main objective is to stay in Bentley's good graces."

"That was three sentences," Tyler deadpanned.

"Jeez, I'm trying here," Andrea said, laughing. "OK, I'll try again. Tim Russell is the VP of Finance, and really, he's an OK accountant, but he's watching the clock and looking forward to retirement."

"Better, but kind of a run-on sentence," Tyler said, smirking.

"Try to live with it," Andrea said. "Um, Sammi Wright, in charge of HR, is from Jamaica and really a nice person and knows her stuff, but it's all people management related and she virtually has no experience with the kinds of business decisions that we'll have to make."

"So she's deadweight?"

"No! No, not at all. She does a good job of hiring and keeping us in compliance with all the HR laws, but it's not like she's going to have any ideas about cutting costs or increasing sales, both of which we need."

Tyler took another long sip of coffee and nodded his understanding. "Who else you got?"

"Robbie Carter is the VP of Logistics. He manages the warehouse, shipping, and receiving, and he makes sure we have supplies and get everything sent out on time."

"No ideas from him either?"

"He talked about trying to shave a day off the average delivery to improve service and maybe cutting back on hours, but he knows that's not enough."

"Well, at least he's a realist," Tyler replied. "Anyone else?"

"Gretchen Hubbard, VP of Sales and Marketing. She's, um, very pleasant and a really good sales person." Andrea stopped there and took a bite of her muffin.

"You damn her with faint praise," Tyler said.

"Well, she's pretty, smart, personable, and a superb sales rep. Just, you know, the next original idea she has will be her first."

"And then there is Andrea Lane."

"Yeah. Me. The Interim VP of Manufacturing whose only here because Bentley is saving money by not replacing my old boss with anyone who would demand higher pay."

Tyler got up from the table and returned with the coffee pot, refilling their cups. "So what are you going to do, Andi?"

Andrea pursed her lips together and shook her head. "I'm sort of stumped. How does one begin on something like this? My ideas to revamp the pay structure of the workers on the line, so they were more motivated, were all nixed by Bentley. That was sort of the crux of what I thought it would take to turn things around. I mean, like you said, the pace of change is increasing and we have to get faster about everything we do. But now, I…I don't know what I can do."

"You wanted to pay them more and you thought that would inspire them to work faster?" Tyler asked.

Andrea reached into her briefcase and pulled out a file. "No. That's how Bentley looks at it, but what I have in mind is not charity. And it's not hopeful optimism that poor performers will suddenly become superstars. Look at this." She pushed a couple of forms in front of her uncle. "See, it's a pay-for-performance model. We pay them a lower base pay and a bonus if they increase production. You know, get more product created so we can get it out the door. If they do the same as what they are doing now, well, they make basically the same amount of money. If they do worse, they make less, but if they do better, they make a lot more. But the reality is we pay them a portion of what would have been profits, but the company actually makes more in real dollars too. And that is what we have to do."

Tyler looked at the diagrams and the numbers. "You believe in this?"

"I do. I've read some books about how to structure the bonus program so everyone feels involved, and it makes perfect sense to me. Right now, we pay everyone just for showing up. How smart can that be when the bank already doesn't like our numbers?"

Tyler nodded. "This is good, Andi. Why don't you just do it anyway?"

"Without Bentley's permission?"

"Why not?" Tyler said. "Look, the company is in a death spiral. You're going to lose your job anyway, so go out fighting."

"The CFO, Tim, will never approve the bonuses. He's the one who does payroll."

Tyler calmly took another sip of coffee and smiled wickedly. "How much in savings have you got?"

"Not six million dollars," Andrea said, eyeing him suspiciously.

"Go to Bentley, tell him to give you three months of a test run. In return, offer to work for twenty percent less. If he doesn't like the results, tell him you'll resign."

Andrea almost choked on her coffee. "What? I can't do that! Then I'll be unemployed and broke too."

"You said you believed in it."

"I do," Andrea replied.

"Then put your money where your mouth is."

"Easy for you to say," Andrea tossed back at him.

"I know, I know," Tyler said softly. "But a few years ago, I left a tenured post with the university, making $150K per year and hardly having to break a sweat for it. I left it for this." He swept his right arm around the bar. "It was scary, but I believed I would learn more here: about people, about the world, about business, and about myself. And I have. It turned out to be the best thing I ever did."

Tyler turned back to his coffee and let her stew on that thought for a while. After a few minutes, he said, "Let's talk about the world we're in. Give you some perspective."

Andrea just nodded, her eyes giving him permission to go on.

"Regarding business, I believe there are three truths about this world we live in. The first is that the pace of change will continue to increase faster and faster. Nothing will be static or stagnant for very long again. The second is that it's going to happen no matter what. It will happen whether we embrace it, despise it, or ignore it. The truth is, we are all along for the ride. It's bigger than any one of us, and we are powerless to change that."

Andrea nodded slowly, trying to fully grasp his meaning. "OK, that's two. You said there were three truths."

"The third is that you can do more than you think. Embrace the change and make it work for you. Those who fight it will lose. Stand still and the world will pass you by. You may be powerless to stop it, but you aren't powerless to gain from it."

"I get it," Andrea said. "But this is all kind of theoretical. I agree with you, but I still don't understand what I can do to make things better. I mean, what I can specifically do. Are you saying you think my incentive plan will be enough?"

"Not at all. You'll need more than that, but it's a big step in the right direction. Here, I want you to take a look at these two pictures." Tyler reached into his folder and removed two pictures. One showed two people sitting in a rickety rowboat paddling down a river. The other showed a college team of rowers in a sleek racing boat, all with their oars rowing in unison.

"Look at both pictures. If these two boats were in a race, who do you suppose would win?"

Andrea looked back at her uncle and chuckled. "Well, pretty obviously, the crew in the racing boat."

"Yes. It seems obvious, doesn't it? Yet so many businesses don't get it. You see, you have to build a team and get them all working together and rowing in the same direction. You can't win the race alone. The first big step is to build a team. You can start with all the line workers in manufacturing and prove to the others that getting everyone into the same boat is the only way to win. What do you do *now*? You start building that team. And that starts from the bottom up."

MONDAY, JANUARY 29

Monday afternoon found Andrea in her office outlining the main points she wanted to make when she addressed the manufacturing department's employees. Most of the morning had been taken up by her meeting with Bentley. She made her bold offer to him and when she was done, he took out his notepad and started scribbling notes to himself. Andrea was at once mortified and ecstatic. Bentley had several tells, and one was taking notes. He only did that when he liked an idea and was getting closer to agreeing to it. Andrea found herself both fearful and excited at the same time.

After doing the math and making an unhappy face, he said, "I'm not sold on those ideas of yours and your offer doesn't save me much money. I just want to get everyone more productive. I don't want you experimenting and changing everything with my company."

"Sir, with all due respect, we've been trying the same old things for years and productivity always stays right about the same level. We have to do something different, something more aggressive. I am certain my plan will work, but we have to move fast. This is the time to do it. If not, we may not even be in business six months from now."

"I'm sure if we just make a good effort the bank will come through for us," Bentley said.

"And you want to bet the whole company on that idea?" Andrea asked.

Bentley hesitated. He rubbed his chin.

Sensing this may be her last play, Andrea said, "Mr. Bentley, I am one hundred percent positive that I can do this and that the changes I suggested will bump up productivity immediately. I'll agree to take a *fifty* percent pay cut for the next three months. If, after that time, you're not happy with the results, I'll resign."

"Fifty percent, huh? You ever done this before?"

"Not exactly," Andrea replied. She quickly followed it up with something more positive. "But I've read a lot: some case studies, some theory. I'm sure it will work for us too."

Bentley sat back down at his desk and stared out the window. Time seemed to stand still for Andrea, and just as she was feeling unable to wait any longer, Bentley picked up his pen and started writing.

When he finished, he said, "I'll give you two months, that's it. If I don't like the results, I'll accept your resignation." He handed her the three-sentence note he had written.

I, Andrea Lane, have permission to experiment with an alternate compensation system for the workers in the Manufacturing Department. I agree to a 50 percent reduction in my pay during those two months. If management is unhappy with my results, I agree to resign immediately.

He drew a line underneath for Andrea to sign on and smiled back at her.

"Do your worst," he said.

Recognizing that phrase as the closest Bentley would ever come to verbal praise, she signed and asked for a copy.

Not anxious to do any work himself, he handed it to her and told her to make her own copy and bring back the original to him. "And while you're at it, run three copies for my secretary, um, Joan…" He paused for a moment, thinking.

"You mean JoAnn?" Andrea asked.

"Yes, and tell her to put a copy in an envelope, make it out for my attorney, and stamp it, and then I want you to run it directly to the post office."

Pointing to her chest, Andrea said, "Excuse me, did you say you wanted *me* to run it to the post office?"

"You're holding the stopwatch, aren't ya?" Bentley answered.

Andrea gave a weak smile and a nod before leaving the room, shaking her head.

After returning to her office, she finished up with her speech bullet points and felt the pit in her stomach widening. *What have I done? In two months, I could be both unemployed and broke.*

A knock on her open door snapped her out of her reverie.

Robbie Carter smiled back at her from the door and asked, "Deep in thought?"

"Yeah. I was wondering what I got myself into. What's up, Robbie?"

"Well, it wasn't exactly a secret you were in with the boss for almost two hours. So that's my question for you—what's up?"

"It wasn't that long. I laid out my plan for getting the employees more involved by starting a bonus program and he finally agreed to it."

Eyebrows arching, Robbie asked, "He agreed? How did you do that?"

"I made him an offer he couldn't refuse," Andrea replied, only half-kidding.

Intrigued now, Robbie asked, "What are you gonna do?"

"Tell you what, it's almost four o'clock. I told the crew to knock off at four so I can talk to them all and have their undivided attention. We're meeting down on the floor in ten minutes. Why don't you come on down and listen in?"

"OK," Robbie said, drawing out the two-syllable word much longer than it deserved.

"Give me a few minutes, Robbie. I just have one more thing to figure out and it's really got me stumped."

"What is it? Maybe I can help," Robbie offered.

Andrea shook her head. "I don't know. The changes I'm proposing are major and it won't really make sense to people unless I tell them the truth—you know, the stuff about closing down in six months if we don't improve."

"Ugh," Robbie said, making a face. "I thought about that too. We all promised not to say anything."

"Yeah," Andrea said, nodding. "But there has to be some sense of urgency or nobody will like what I have to say."

"You know," Robbie said, rubbing his chin. "I did have one idea about that. I was trying to figure out how to get my warehouse crew motivated, so I came up with something. You might like to use it."

"Time's a-wastin', Robbie. Tell me!"

Robbie shared his idea, and ten minutes later, Andrea found herself on the floor near the head of Line 3, notes in her hand, waiting for everyone to get seated. As they took their seats, she flashed back, remembering an article saying that a speech like the one she was about to give needed to be well articulated and, preferably, a bit inspiring. It had to explain the reasons change is necessary, the challenges and opportunities ahead, and paint a picture of how making those changes would impact the employees in a good way. She swallowed hard.

Great. Wouldn't want to make this too easy on me.

When every chair was filled and the room grew silent, Andrea started in. "You all know me and you all know I care about the quality of our work and I care about each of you. You also know I don't generally exaggerate good news or bad news. I just tell it like it is. And right now, well, it's not so great. I'm here to tell you that our competition, people like Murphy's GardenWare and SQT Lawn and Garden, have ramped up, improved their speed of delivery, and are kicking our butts right now. Big time. Our sales have dipped slightly, but most importantly, our speed of output has fallen too, so we tend to be slower with delivery and new products and features. In other words, the competition is winning and we're not. And we desperately need to do something about it."

She stopped to take a breath, and one of the workers called out, "There gonna be layoffs?"

Immediately, Andrea shook her head and said, "Not right now, but let's be real: if this keeps up, there will be. We have time to turn it around, but we have to do something completely different. I know that no one likes sudden change, but I believe that this is a change you'll grow to like very much. Effective February 1st, we are going to institute a new pay scale that will give you the opportunity to make more every month than you are right now."

For the next fifteen minutes, Andrea explained how pay would basically remain the same but the reasons they are getting paid would change. She explained that base pay would be reduced by 10 percent and replaced with a bonus program that paid everyone back that same 10 percent if normal levels of production were met. If they weren't, everyone would get a smaller bonus and it could be slightly less than what they had lost. However, if they did exceed the goal, they would get a pro-rated amount higher—potentially far higher—than what they used to be paid.

She handed out a one-page flyer with the February goals and rewards highlighted on it.

<u>The February Bonus Program</u>

Everyone will get the bonus amounts shown below if we produce enough units to reach the first, the middle, or the top goal.

FIRST GOAL: 3,400 units   PAYROLL BONUS: $300

MIDDLE GOAL: 3,650 units   PAYROLL BONUS: $400

TOP GOAL: 4,000 units   PAYROLL BONUS: $600

Making our first goal requires only an average of 170 units per day, a bit higher than we normally do, but not nearly as much as we are capable of doing. We will post the rising totals every day so you all know how you are doing.

Utilizing a helpful caveat she read about, she reminded every-one that it is hard to design the perfect bonus program on the very first try, so she may have to tweak it to make sure it rewarded everyone fairly.

She allowed thirty minutes for questions and answers and found the employees had a high level of skepticism. Most were focused on the base pay decrease and the penalty of lower productivity rather than the joys of working hard and making much more money. She fielded questions for close to ninety minutes, marveling at how the employees were willing to stay after the five o'clock horn sounded to delve deeper into the issues.

By six o'clock, Andrea was back in her office, exhausted from the experience. Robbie looked equally exhausted, even though all he had done was listen.

She collapsed into her chair and made eye contact with her fellow VP. "That was harder than I thought. Did you hear all their questions? They hated the idea. They don't trust management at all."

"I'm not sure I blame them. Bentley hasn't exactly endeared himself to anyone," Robbie replied.

"I know. But I thought some of them would like the idea of a team goal and could start thinking about the upside of making more money."

Robbie got up to leave. "Well, Andrea, for what it's worth, I like the idea. And I think you may be the bravest exec I've met around here. At least you're trying. I think the rest love this work but have given up already. I admire what you're doing."

Fighting to keep her jaw from dropping to the floor, Andrea replied, "Um, thanks, Robbie. That means a lot to me. It's been a while since I've heard positive words...of any kind, around here."

Robbie nodded, smiled, and waved good-bye.

Heading home, Andrea detoured to Delano Street and parked a half block away from Uncle Tyler's Bar. She entered amid a busy crowd and got Tyler's attention.

He turned over his work to a bartender and came in her direction. "What's up, Andi?"

"Jeez, sorry, you're busy. I was gonna talk, but maybe we'll make it another time."

"I have three bartenders here tonight. They can get by without my brilliant management guidance for a few minutes. Talk to me."

"Well," Andrea began, "I got Bentley to agree to my terms, except he didn't think my offer of twenty percent was enough, so I offered to cut my pay by *fifty* percent, and he only gave me two months instead of three. Then I had a meeting with all the manufacturing employees and explained the new bonus program."

"Let me guess," Tyler said. "They hated it."

"Yes! I thought they'd be excited about the chance to make more money and—"

Tyler cut her off. "Honey, it's human nature. Man is moved by two levers only—fear and self-interest. Napoleon said that, and I'm not sure truer words have ever been spoken. You tried to appeal to their self-interest, but all they could feel was the fear."

"But you liked my idea," Andrea said, a bit of a whine in her voice.

"I did. And I do. And now you have the honor and privilege of trying to make radical change in a ridiculously short period of time. You haven't had time to develop trust and confidence and credibility with all these people yet, but you have to do it anyway. It's still a good plan, but their reaction is predictable."

"I might need a drink," Andrea said.

Tyler laughed. "Nah. Too soon for that thought. You're doing fine. You've got more nerve than ninety percent of all the execs out there. Now you have to move on to the second stage."

"And what would that be?"

"Now is when you fight for their hearts and minds. You have to make them trust you and believe in you," Tyler said with a smile.

"Oh, is that all. And how do you propose I do that?"

Tyler grew serious and looked her in the eye. "Be genuine. Be real. Be empathetic, and work your brains out to make this successful. I believe in you. You can do it."

Andrea stared back at him and slowly nodded her head. "I…I can do it," she repeated uncertainly.

She turned to leave but suddenly stopped. "Wait a minute. I came here to find out one more thing. Saturday morning you said the blueberry muffin was a good business lesson and that we'd come back to it, but we never did."

Tyler smiled, seemingly happy that she remembered. "I knew you'd come back to it when you were ready. Tell me, why did you feel happy when you saw that I'd made a special effort to get that muffin for you?"

"Well, obviously, it was a nice thing to do. But it took you time. That bakery is always packed and I know how much you hate to stand in line. But you did it. You did it for *me*. It made me feel special."

Tyler just looked at her.

Andrea stared back and said, "Oh, jeez, you're doing that thing again where you expect some bolt of lightning to come down and…and…"

"Did it hit you yet?"

"I should do the same thing for the employees. I should do whatever it takes to convince them I care and that…that they are special. Right?"

"*Do* you care, Andrea?"

"I do. I *do* care. They have families. My God, closing the plant would devastate them."

Tyler nodded. "Good. Because you can't fake it. They'll smell insincerity a mile away. But if you really care, you have to fight for them. You have to show them how special they are. Every day, you have to give them that same feeling you got from seeing that muffin. And the beauty of it all is that it's the simple things like saying 'thank you' when someone does a good job or giving a thumbs-up 'atta boy!' at the right moment. It won't happen overnight. Some will always mistrust you, but if you are genuine, most of them will start believing in you."

Mulling that over, she replied, "Well, it'll certainly make me different from the other VPs. They mostly treat their employees like a commodity rather than flesh-and-blood human beings."

"That's the problem. Those employees don't want to get in your boat. And if they do, they secretly try to row the wrong way. Bosses who treat their people that way don't get it. The best boss gets good results by being the servant. Give them everything they need to do a good job and serve them. That's how you win."

FRIDAY, FEBRUARY 2

Tim Russell arrived at Brannigan's Pub and joined Robbie and Gretchen at the table for six. Before he was in his seat, he was telling them about his day. "The Finance Department was slammed from every side today. Bentley wanted a projected cash flow statement for next month, the bank wanted backup docs on, well, everything, and I had to cut my lunch meeting with some old friends short just to get it all done." He took a deep breath and stared at the other two, waiting for their condolences.

"I was busy all day too," Gretchen said. "Had a sales meeting and then had to help Larry prepare his presentation for Walmart. He is so nervous. I feel like I oughta do it for him." She looked over at Robbie as though it were his turn to complain.

Realizing they were both waiting for him to say something, Robbie added, "Same ole, same ole in shipping. Every day seems busy."

As he finished his sentence, Andrea walked in the door with Sammi and Craig. They spotted the others quickly and seated themselves.

Craig, VP of Ops, took control of the meeting and said, "All right, let's try to make this brief. I have a life even if you others don't."

"I'm all for brief," Tim agreed.

Andrea just looked at them and shook her head. Speaking in a low tone so nearby tables didn't hear her, she said, "Guys, we're going to have all the time in the world to do anything we please in about five months when we go out of business. If we're going to save our jobs and everybody else's too, we have to agree on some changes and start making them happen fast. That might take some time and—"

"This isn't your meeting," Craig said, cutting her off. "You don't get to run things here."

"Craig, we're here after hours, having a beer," Robbie said. "We don't need Robert's Rules of Order here. This is supposed to be a voluntary discussion. Anybody can speak."

"I'm used to running things," Craig said with a tinge of a whine in his voice. "There has to be some organization to this or we'll be here all night."

Sammi and Gretchen looked to Andrea.

Catching their eyes, Andrea said, "Craig, I just don't think we can rush this. We're all in new territory here. Let's just let the conversation flow. I mean, I for one would like to know what Bentley said to everybody's proposals they gave him. I think we all need to be aware of what the other departments are doing so we work together better."

"I agree," Sammi chimed in. "I'll start. I gave Bentley a laundry list of changes we could make in HR and he said he'd think on it. I mean, most of my ideas cost more money than what we are doing now, but frankly, we're hardly doing anything."

"He's thinking on it. That's progress," Tim said.

Andrea and Sammi rolled their eyes.

"Tim, every day counts. Bentley just never seems to want to do anything different. How are we going to improve if all he ever does is think on it?" Andrea asked.

Tim shook his head. "You don't understand. Running a business is complicated. I applaud his steady style of management."

Robbie jumped into the fray. "Tim, what did the Finance Department suggest to Bentley?"

Tim sipped his beer and said, "I told him I thought we should push harder for a lower interest rate on the existing loans and I'm going to squeeze all our vendors to lower their prices."

"And?" Andrea asked.

"And what?" Tim replied.

"Did Bentley agree to any of that?"

"Well, we can't put much pressure on the bank right now. The interest rate idea has to wait until we negotiate the next loan. But he did agree that I could play hardball with the vendors, and I'm going to insist on lower rates from them, and if they don't comply, I'll stretch out payment terms to ninety days instead of the current sixty."

That set off a firestorm of protest from Robbie, Andrea, and Gretchen, who could see the vendor pressure resulting in lower quality products, shipment delays, and worsening vendor relations. The rest of the meeting went downhill from there.

Saturday morning, Andrea showed up at the Professor's Bar and Grill at eight o'clock for what was becoming a traditional Saturday planning session with Uncle Tyler.

Again, he had a blueberry muffin for her as well as a plate of fresh fruit, coffee, and orange juice.

They ate and talked as Andrea filled him in on the VP meeting at Brannigan's.

Tyler listened attentively, then tried to summarize. "So you're telling me that none of the other VPs got any agreement from Bentley to do anything?"

"He's thinking. Apparently, he does a lot of that."

Tyler shook his head. "He doesn't have time to think. OK, wait, that didn't sound right either. But, really, he needs to take action. You got him to agree to *your* plan."

"I had to promise to agree to a monster pay cut, and in two months, if he doesn't like the results, I'm toast, remember? Some really clever business guru talked me into putting my money where my mouth is," Andrea said, only half-kidding.

"I remember. A genius plan if I ever heard one," Tyler said, laughing. "Of course, I only suggested twenty percent, not half. But, seriously, it'll be fine. It'll work and he'll love it. But apparently he didn't love anybody else's plan."

"There's a common thread," Andrea said. "If it cost money, any money more than what we are spending now, it needs a lot more thought. Meanwhile, time is slipping away. I'm counting weeks now. We've got twenty-two left before the bank will want to see what we did."

"He's not going to do anything, is he?" Tyler asked.

"I doubt it. So I'm doubling down. After Tim and Craig left last night, I told Sammi, Robbie, and Gretchen what I'm going to do next. You wanna hear it?"

"Absolutely. I like it when you talk and I can listen. It's easier to eat that way. Tell me how you're doubling down."

Andrea chuckled. "OK, but you'll probably think I'm crazy. See, I'm going to follow some other advice you've given me over the years. I'm going to go ahead and change the way we do performance reviews, and I'm not asking Bentley's permission. I'll ask his forgiveness later."

"I like it already."

"It's kinda radical," Andrea said as she helped herself to a pineapple wedge.

"Tell me."

"I've been reading about a seriously different way to evaluate performance and make raise decisions. I told Sammi—you know, the VP of Human Resources—and she said she liked it. And it's not illegal."

"That's comforting," Tyler replied.

"I'm going to announce it to the crew on Monday. I'm delinking performance reviews and pay raise decisions."

Tyler almost choked as he hurriedly finished chewing his mouthful. "Come again? What?"

"We have to speed everything up, right? And we have to get people on the same page. Fast! Do you know how much time and energy goes into preparing a performance review and then making a decision on whether or not they get a raise and how much it will be?"

"I know, at the University, it always took me too long," Tyler said.

"That's the correct answer for everyone," Andrea said. "It always takes *too* long. I've got ninety-two employees in the Manufacturing Department and we do yearly reviews. In February alone, we're scheduled to give eleven of them."

"OK, so what's the alternative? The employees still expect their yearly increase, don't they? You'll have a revolt on your hands if you don't give it to them."

"They'll get their raises," Andrea said. "Well, they'll get what they deserve."

"You're just going to give them some kind of raise, but no review," Tyler asked, apprehensively.

"Sort of. Let me tell you how this concept works. Feel free to stuff your face while I chatter on."

"Perfect," Tyler agreed.

"First of all," Andrea began, "it's not like the current once-a-year-review-and-a-raise is the supremely best system we could ever design. In fact, it's downright terrible. It's one of the most demotivating exercises anyone could imagine. I mean, really, the employee sweats and worries about the review for months before it's given. The manager struggles for far too many hours to create an accurate review and lessen his own concerns because it is such an antagonistic process to go through. No one wants to tell someone, or hear from someone, all their faults and weaknesses. The employee gets all defensive and so does the boss. Consequently, many reviewers just take the easy way out and don't give the employee good feedback because it's no fun being the bad guy. Then they announce that the employee is going to get a three percent raise, or five percent or whatever. And it's never enough! It's never as much as the employee expected or hoped for. Never! So now the manager has spent far too many hours creating the review and making the pay decision and the employee feels underappreciated and underpaid. Congratulations! That's how we motivate people with reviews and yearly raises in America."

Tyler smeared a bit of red jelly on his face as he tried to gulp down the last bite of his donut.

"Really, I'm not trying to make a joke about the process. And please be careful, you're getting some of that in your mouth," Andrea said as she smiled and pointed to his lips.

"Everybody's a critic. Keep going. I want to hear more about this, Andi."

Andrea chuckled at her own joke, then grew deadly serious. "OK, I know it sounds weird, but the goal of a review is to inform the employee how management perceives their performance, to help them improve, and to motivate them to do better by giving them a commensurate raise. And, honestly, no one ever gets told they are getting no raise at all. So it's always *some* amount, and for the poor performers, they get so little that they are mad, embarrassed, humiliated, and totally unmotivated."

She rose from her seat and stood, as though she were making a formal presentation. Tyler noted how animated she had become and remembered she always expressed herself better when standing up.

Andrea was off and running. "On top of that, yearly reviews create a massive amount of angst. The typical employee goes into the review thinking they really need X percent of a raise or their personal goals are shot. They might need the money to buy a house or send a kid to school, and if they don't get enough, they either have to get a second job or wait until next year. Are you kidding me? That's their plan—wait till next year? How does that make them feel?"

Not waiting for an answer, she continued, "So they go into the review carrying all these extra hopes and dreams, and do you think for a minute they are actually listening to what the boss is saying? Of course they aren't. All they can think about is, 'C'mon, get this review part over with and tell me how much I get.' A review is a terrible forum for a frank conversation. And when they get heated and both sides are shouting at each other because the boss said something that offended the employee, how much quality communication is really going on there? The whole process sucks."

"OK," Tyler said slowly, measuring his words. "What's the alternative?"

"Delink. I'll tell everyone that from now on, we will not be announcing pay raise amounts during the review. And further, reviews will be replaced by informal coaching sessions. We'll talk with employees when they are on the line or briefly in our office, or wherever we are, about how they can improve so they can make more money. Now I'm not reviewing. I'm not critiquing. I'm *coaching*. I'm helping them make more money."

Tyler wiped his face with a napkin and said, "OK, but I'm still not sure—"

Andrea put her hand up in the stop position. "I'm not done yet. Have another donut."

Tyler laughed and obeyed her.

"Here's the tricky part. I create a spreadsheet with fifteen columns. The employee name goes in the first column, their anniversary date in the second, with their current pay rate in the third. The rest are the twelve months of the year. If an employee is up for a yearly review, like our eleven who were hired in some previous February, I consider each of them and decide how much to give them, if anything. Then I *don't* schedule any meetings X weeks into the future so the employee can lose sleep, sweat, and get all worked up waiting for the day. Instead, I just call them into my office one day and say, 'Brenda, you're doing really well on your daily job on Line 6. I'm raising you up by fifty dollars per month starting immediately. Work on getting here to start the day on time more often and I know you'll see another raise.'"

Andrea paused for a moment and smiled at her uncle.

"But...but, Andi, wouldn't she have expected more than fifty dollars a month for the yearly raise?"

"Well, yes, but this is diff—" Andrea replied.

Tyler interrupted her. "Well, I think you have to address that issue."

"It's not a *yearly* raise anymore, Unc. It's an *anytime* raise. That changes the whole dynamics of it. What do you know about the four recognized schedules of reinforcement?"

Tyler's eyebrows arched and he replied, "About as much as I know about Australian water polo."

"Oh, cool, for once I can teach you something. OK, I'm just going to hit the highlights. There are four different types of reinforcement: fixed ratio, fixed interval, variable ratio, and variable interval. One of those four has been proven to be *far* more motivating than the other three."

Continuing on with hardly a pause for breath, Andrea said, "So you have **fixed ratio**—the employee gets a raise after a consistent and preset number of times he does something right. Usually that means showing up for work or finishing, say, ten thousand successful steps on the assembly line. **Fixed interval** is what we do now—the employee gets a raise once a year.

"**Variable ratio** is when the employee gets a raise after she performs a changing, but specific, number of actions, and **variable interval** is when the employee gets a raise after doing well throughout a random period of time. Scientific studies on animals and humans have proven that the subject is most motivated to perform when reinforcement is given over random intervals. And I mean *way* more motivated."

"So, to get people to work hard," Andrea continued, "and give it their best every day, management should give positive reinforcement using variable interval reinforcement—that is, raises at random intervals. That solves the problem that the yearly raise creates—employees bringing their game up a month or so before raise time and then slacking off again after getting the raise because they know they can't get any more money for another year. When you reward on the variable interval schedule, people bring their A game to work every day."

Tyler mulled that over and slowly said, "I guess I'm still not getting it. In your example, you said you looked at the employees on your chart that were due for a raise in February, their anniversary month. So how is that different?"

"Sorry," Andrea replied, "I didn't make that clear. I'm thinking about me and how I would start it up. I'd have to start with those folks who expected a raise anyway or I'd have a riot on my hands. But then after that, I key in on whoever is experiencing an anniversary month, but I also look at everyone on the chart. Once a month I simply go down the line of employees and ask myself if that person is doing well enough for a reinforcement raise in that month. If they are, I make a note on the form of how much I increased their pay and I let them know."

Andrea paused for a moment, then started again, "This is the fun part. Instead of having this angst-ridden review moment in my office with the employee, I simply pull them aside or have them come in to see me and I surprise them with the raise. I tell them what they are doing that I like and I give them a suggestion on what they could improve on to get another raise. That means virtually every day that someone comes in to work could be a day when they get a raise. And since they know there is no set time interval, they could get a raise twice in the same month or two in three months or whatever. And the raises don't have to be huge. They can be small or medium and it's never bad news—it's only *good* because A, they didn't expect it, and B, they know they could get another one very soon. That's what motivates."

Tyler nodded. "Don't forget the blueberry muffins."

Andrea laughed. "Yes, that too. I mean, I still have to do the touchy-feely things and gain their trust and understanding, but when employees start hearing that everyone around them is getting called into the office and handed a raise, that should convince them that it's real and that they can trust us to reward them when they do well. Every time we hand out a raise, it'll build our credibility."

"What if someone is not doing so great? Then what?" Tyler asked.

"I think then it becomes clearer who is helping the team and who isn't. I can still have a coaching session with them and give them very specific goals that they need to achieve in order to get a raise. I tell them what they have to improve on to make more money, but it might be that this kind of method will help those folks to realize they need to bring it up a notch or find a new career. When everyone else is getting raises and you're not, that would make you think, right?"

Tyler nodded his agreement. "The current way, the one-re-view-a-year way, those guys are skating because most managers will just give them a modest increase and the employee will take it so they can hang on to their job."

"I think so," Andrea agreed. "We're rewarding them for show-ing up, but for all we know, they are making everybody else's job more difficult because they're not pulling their weight."

Tyler chuckled and said, "You know, I like it. I really didn't think about it, but I'm doing the same thing here with my wait-ers and bartenders. I mean, I don't have a spreadsheet or a formal game plan, but when I get a good employee that I want to keep around, I raise his pay right away. It's a real meritocracy and the better workers get paid more. It's just harder to do that with a big company, isn't it?"

"It is," Andrea concurred. "But like I said, we're not union-ized so it's not illegal. We'd still be compensating people, but we'd be doing it for different reasons, and with the bonus program too, we're paying them truly for performance and not just for showing up and clocking in. It's sort of a one-two punch."

"You know what else will happen," Tyler said, warming to the idea. "When somebody gets a surprise raise and they go home that night, they get to tell their significant other, 'Hey, I got a raise today!' and it doesn't matter if it's a small raise. It wasn't expected so it's all positive. They're not coming home after a formal yearly review and complaining about management's harsh perception of their performance and the yearly raise they got that wasn't enough."

"I know," Andrea agreed. "And I'm betting that a happy work crew is the first step in getting everyone into that boat with me and rowing the same way."

Tyler stared at her for a moment and quietly asked, "You're really going to do this?"

Andrea nodded her head. "I'm going to explain it all to them on Monday."

"They're going to hate it, you know."

Andrea swallowed hard. "I know. They won't trust me."

"They already don't trust the company," Tyler added. "Bentley's never given them any reason to. You haven't got enough credibility with them yet to convince them it will work."

Andrea nodded. "I'm all in. I'm betting everything that they'll trust me soon. I'll just have to demonstrate it to them."

They picked up their empty plates and moved them to the kitchen. Andrea gave her uncle a hug and headed for the door.

As she opened it, Tyler called out, "Andrea, you got a tough road ahead. I sure wish Bentley had given you three months instead of two."

Again, Andrea nodded. She waved and said, "See you soon."

As the door closed behind her, Tyler shook his head and whispered to himself, "Atta girl."

MONDAY, FEBRUARY 5TH

Early Monday morning, Andrea arrived before everyone else and set up two tables in the Manufacturing Division. She placed a dozen boxes of mixed donuts on the table, as well as two canisters of coffee and one of hot water. She left a generous number of tea bags there along with napkins and paper plates. She posted a sign saying, *FOR OUR AMAZING MANUFACTURING TEAM!*

She picked a bear claw for herself, grabbed a cup of fully caffeinated coffee, and headed for her office, where she planned to outline the points she was going to make at tonight's 4:30 meeting.

During the day, she had a meeting with Sammi to confirm that Human Resources would support her radical pay raise procedures and stopped by the warehouse to say hi to Robbie.

"Hey, you guys look busy this morning," she called out to the Logistics VP as she climbed up onto the dock.

"We're down a couple guys today so everyone's gotta hustle," Robbie replied as he lifted a load onto a pallet. "What's up?"

"Nothing, really," Andrea replied. "I stopped to see Sammi and then was just down this way, so I thought I'd stop in."

Robbie eyed her. "Sammi's office is on the other side of the building."

Caught in her lie, Andrea chuckled and said, "Yeah, I know. I was, you know, meandering. I'm getting nervous about tonight.

I was wondering, would you care to sit in on the meeting and see what you can see and hear? Maybe give me some feedback later?"

"What time?"

"I'm starting at 4:30," Andrea said.

Robbie rubbed his chin and nodded. "I got a lot to do here, but I'd like to see how they react. I've been thinking I might do something similar. I'll try to be there."

Andrea's face erupted into a smile. "Thanks. See you around."

She headed back to her office and prepared for the meeting. She met with each of the three line supervisors and explained the new process to them and discussed their new roles. When she finished those meetings, she polished up her outline until she was certain she had her key points memorized.

A half hour before the end of the shift, Andrea sounded the bell early and stood in front of the ninety-two employees of the Manufacturing Department.

Some of the employees in the room were straining their necks to see her, so Andrea moved a few steps up the stairway to gain some height and create a better view. She took a second to make eye contact with those workers. "Good afternoon, everyone. As I mentioned, we are knocking off thirty minutes early so I can fill you in on some other tactics and procedures we've decided to try to help ourselves gain back some business we've been losing to the competitors.

"One of the issues I'm concerned about is our procedure for giving reviews and rewarding employees with higher pay for good performance. The way we do it now is that everyone gets one hour-long performance review per year and we assign a new pay rate if we feel the employee merits it. I don't know about you, but generally this isn't my favorite task. It's contentious, kinda scary, nerve wracking for both parties, and simply not a lot of fun. It also takes up a considerable amount of time for everyone, and I'm not at all convinced it does a good job of rewarding people properly.

"So, after some long conversations with the HR Department, they've agreed to let the Manufacturing Division try out a new system. In this new system, our goal is to continually give feedback to all employees but in less rigid and structured methods. Fact is, your Line Supervisors—Malik, Meghan, and Charlie—and I will make every effort to constantly be talking to you about what you can improve on and what you're already doing that is really good and may not need any improvement. It will be more in the line of coaching instead of critiquing, and it will also help us identify who is ready for a raise."

A few of the employees raised their hands, and one called out, "I don't get what the difference is?"

Turning his way, Andrea replied, "What's different is that in this new system, we are discarding the procedure of once-a-year reviews and once-a-year raises. Instead we will give frequent coaching tips, and as we see people performing well and improving those issues brought up in the coaching sessions, we will grant raises pretty much on the spot. In our new system, it will be possible to get a raise in February and another one in March or April. Or, for that matter, any other time that an employee demonstrates rapid improvement or shows the ability to take on more tasks. So raises will probably be smaller than your once-a-year raises may have been, but they will be more frequent and more related to your current performance."

Andrea stopped and looked out at the crowd, trying to judge their reaction. She spotted Robbie in the back, watching closely.

"We really believe that you'll like this system better and it will reward you in a more appropriate—"

"Yeah! We get it," one of the workers on Line 5 called out, interrupting her. "This is your way of screwing us and making it sound good. This is how the company plans to compete—work us harder for less money and then take away our guaranteed yearly raises, too."

Andrea listened to him and glanced at Meghan, the Lines 5 and 6 supervisor. She mouthed his name and Andrea nodded back.

"Stan, I can understand why you think that, but I am standing here assuring you that is not the case."

"Yeah?" Stan yelled back immediately. "What about all the guys here, like Ricky? February is his review month and he is counting on his raise. Now he's not getting one? And no review either? Sounds like a crummy deal for all of us."

"Everyone is going to participate in this new system," Andrea replied, "and we are specifically zeroing in on those employees who have gone longest between raises. The transition to this system can't be totally cold turkey. We have to smoothly segue a bit into it, but the same rules will apply to everyone, and I am confident that when we do this, you will grow more comfortable with it and realize how you can basically give yourself a raise simply by working hard to improve. I'm asking everyone to give this a chance and judge it on its own merits."

A worker on Line 2 raised his hand and said, "Last week, you announced you were lowering our base pay and putting us on a bonus program that pays us the same as before but only if we make the goal for the month. Now you're messing with our raises. Looks to me like this is a money grab by the suits in the head office."

Andrea shook her head. "I'm not going to sugarcoat this. We are getting our butts seriously kicked by the competition, and unless we do something different, we will have far worse problems than these. That being said, I believe we have the best workforce in the industry right here and we can beat those guys back and claim the lead again. We just can't do it by doing everything as we always have. We have to modernize and give everyone a greater stake and a greater reward for success. These two major changes will give us the best chance to do that."

She looked around. None of the heads were nodding their agreement and the smiles were nonexistent. "Today is the fifth of February, and so far this month, we've produced 358 completed units for sale. Our monthly average is about 3,650. That would be what we normally get done, and I think we need to focus on the positive rather than the negative. We beat that goal and charge after the next one and you can put more bonus money in your pockets and you'll have the opportunity to earn higher base pay multiple times during the year. I believe in this plan, and please remember, three months ago, I was a supervisor on the lines and two years before that, I worked those same lines just as you do. I get it. I know how much every dollar means to you, and I promise you, this is no plan to earn more profits off your hard work. If we do earn more, you will too."

Carol Womack, a worker in Line 1, called out, "I say Andrea's been straight with us before. I say we give it a try for a few months."

Resisting the urge to go down and hug the life out of Carol, Andrea replied, "That's all I'm asking. If I'm wrong and this doesn't work—if it fails to make you feel like you are being treated more fairly—then I have no doubt I will lose my job long before you do. I believe in you and in your potential, so I'm betting everything I've got that you'll succeed."

Stan stood up and boomed out again, "You talk a good game, Andrea, but I'm not buying it. Mark my word, this is just another management bullshit move to make more money by screwing us."

Without waiting an extra second for someone to second that motion, Andrea called out, "Time will tell. I still believe you'll like this. Thank you for your attention. My door is open to anyone who wants to talk. It's 4:55, so go ahead and punch out and we'll see everyone tomorrow."

The room started to clear, and Andrea left to return to her office. Three minutes later, Robbie stuck his head in her door.

"That went about like I thought it might," Robbie offered.

Andrea rolled her eyes. "Me too. They hated it. Maybe I moved too fast."

Robbie nodded. "Yeah, I think you did, but that's because you have the guts to do it. Under normal circumstances, you'd probably create some committees of employees to consider the new system and make recommendations and you could prepare people slowly to embrace the change. But these aren't normal conditions, are they?"

Andrea sighed and replied, "No, but we can't tell them that. There really isn't enough time to do this right. I guess I don't see any alternative."

"You embraced the alternative already. The rest of us are slow adapters. I gotta tell you, I've never seen any management person move so fast and so fearlessly."

"You should see me at home. I'm a mess thinking about what I've got to do," Andrea said.

"You didn't look like a mess to me. If I were an employee, you know what you would've looked like?"

Andrea locked eyes with Robbie and softly asked, "What did I look like?"

"You looked like a leader," Robbie said as he headed out. "And people follow leaders. That's what they do."

THURSDAY, FEBRUARY 8

At three o'clock, Andrea checked her schedule and smiled to herself. She was beginning to feel like she was finally catching up on her workload. The three supervisors were due in her office at 3:15 to discuss their lines' performances and make decisions on raises.

Right on time, Malik knocked on her door and she motioned him in. Meghan followed seconds later. Andrea smiled at both of them and said, "Thanks for being so punctual. As soon as Charlie gets here, we'll start up, and I think you can get back on the floor by four thirty."

Meghan glanced at Malik and cleared her throat. Trying hard not to let her facial expressions betray her true feelings, she said, "Um, Charlie's not coming. He said he had a doctor's appointment and he had to leave at two."

"We picked this time two days ago on Tuesday and everybody said they could make it," Andrea said, mostly talking to herself.

Shaking off her disappointment, she wasted no more time on the issue. "Well, we'll tackle Lines 1, 2, 5, and 6, then. I'll deal with Charlie later." Handing them both a piece of paper, she continued, "On this spreadsheet is every employee on your lines, their anniversary date, their current hourly pay, and the months of the year starting with last month, January. You see I already entered the raise amount for the six employees we reviewed in January. Now, let's talk about what we're going to do in February."

Malik and Meghan looked over the reports and saw they each had four employees in their anniversary month.

Meghan, never one to be shy about speaking up, said, "I'm still a little foggy on this. How are we going to do this again? And should we start with the anniversary folks?"

"We'll deal with everyone this month. The anniversary employees will be discussed at another time. Right now, let's talk in more general terms about the process. First, take a look at the first name on your list and ask yourself two questions," Andrea began. "When did he or she get their last raise and have you seen any significant improvement since then? Malik, let's talk this out loud and do your first one together, then we'll do Meghan's."

Malik looked again at his list and said, "The first one is Mike Albers. He, um, his anniversary date is September and his pay rate is $18.80 per hour."

"OK, think back. Did you give him a raise in September?" Andrea asked, coaching him through the process.

"Yeah, I mean we always give a raise of some kind. His was, if I remember right, his was, you know, the average—about a buck."

Andrea stared back at the supervisor. *C'mon, logic it out, Malik.*

Nothing seemed to be happening, so she helped him out. "Well, do you remember what you told him he needed to work on?"

"Yeah, he's late almost every morning. He works just fine, but he can't get here on time. I mean, to his credit, he doesn't fake his timesheet. He shows the real time, but he's like fifteen minutes late every day and it screws up Line 2's pace every morning."

"So you're saying you've seen no improvement since your last review?" Andrea probed.

Malik scrunched up his face and said, "He says it's the bus schedule. I sort of let it be."

"OK, the only remaining question about Mike, then, is should we give him a small raise in February?"

Malik shook his head. "No. No, he's not making any improvement."

"I think that's a very fair analysis," Andrea said, smiling. "We're done with Mike for this month, except for one little thing."

"What's that?" Malik asked, not sure he really wanted to know.

"I think in this case, you need to tell him that we considered him for another raise but since he hasn't improved his punctuality, we passed. Then try to help him make more money. Talk to him about the bus schedule and see if there is any other way, like car-pooling or a different route that would get him in here on time. Tell him he would see a modest pay improvement if he solved that problem."

Malik thought about that and said, "That could take some time."

"Ask him to stay after work and discuss it. Or talk to him on his lunch break. Remember, we aren't critiquing him; we're coaching. We're trying to help him make more money because we win then too."

Meghan smiled and said, "OK, I'm ready. I get it better now."

Andrea looked at her and said, "Who ya got?"

"Sue Anderson. Hired last August. Kind of new. No reviews yet and no raise history."

"How's she doing?" Andrea asked.

"Actually pretty good. She's not the fastest on the line, but she's consistent and she's getting better over time. And she has a good attitude and, you know, she's happy most of the time."

Certain she knew the answer to her next question already, Andrea asked it anyway, "How is being happy important?"

"Well, it is. It just is. It's hard to put your finger on it. But the people around her on the line seem more upbeat too. I think if people like their coworkers and what they are doing and, you know, have a little fun with it, then they stick around longer and the whole line moves smoother."

"Malik, do you agree with that?" Andrea asked.

"Oh yeah. I used to think that wasn't important, but every time I have to hire someone new, I think about all the time it takes me and how long it is before the newbie is up to speed and, believe me, I'm all for cutting down the turnover."

Andrea nodded. "Well, it's not a novel thought, but I think nearly everyone agrees that a happy workforce is a more productive workforce. In fact, we should really be looking for more ways to recognize people and do the little things that help them enjoy their work more. You two are on the right track. Now, back to Sue."

Andrea looked to Meghan, and the supervisor knew that was her cue to discuss the raise issue.

Picking her words slowly, she said, "Andrea, I know we've got to be careful about trying to make everybody happy by handing out raises like candy, but in this case, I think it would mean a lot to her if we bumped her up a bit."

"I think you're right, Meg," Andrea agreed. "I suggest that tomorrow, you call her into your office and tell her you're bumping her pay up effective February 1st."

"Retroactive?"

"Absolutely. It'll only cost us a few bucks more to do that, and it's way better than saying it starts, like, on February 16th or March 1st. I mean, if she's good enough to get a raise, then let's just give it to her. She shouldn't have to wait another one to three weeks. We get more mileage out of it that way."

"How much should I give her?"

"That's an interesting question. First of all, all raises should be expressed as a dollar amount, not a percentage. And the best way to figure it out is to ask yourself if this were her anniversary month and you were giving her a one-year raise, how much do you think you'd give?"

Meghan considered the issue. "Well, she's new, so probably eighty cents an hour or so. Maybe more."

"OK, let's say you're going to raise her pay ninety cents after one year. Her year is up in, what, five and a half months? Think of it as having about a buck to play with. And you can give multiple raises during the year. If you give her ninety cents now, that leaves almost nothing left to work with for the rest of the year unless she improves even more dramatically. My suggestion is that you give her fifty or sixty cents per hour and tell her why, then remind her that you'll be watching and if she can pick up her speed without creating more errors, then you'll be giving her another raise soon."

Meghan made a note to herself on her spreadsheet and said, "OK, so I'm getting it. But won't she be disappointed that she didn't get closer to a dollar?"

Andrea smiled broadly. "No one is going to be disappointed anymore. Well, assuming we gain their trust and they believe in us, that is. This is a surprise raise out of the blue. She doesn't expect it. And it's retroactive, so she's been making more money this whole month without knowing it. Trust me, she'll be pleased."

Meghan smiled too. "It'll be kinda fun to surprise people with good news for a change. But you said to call her into my office. Shouldn't I just tell her right there on the line so everyone else can hear it too?"

"No," Andrea said firmly. "Go up to her, tap her on the shoulder, and say, 'Sue, could you stop by my office for a few minutes just before your next break?' Be sure to say it that way, noncommittally, and do it about fifteen minutes before the break. That way she doesn't have lots of time to worry about it."

Malik shook his head. "I disagree, Andrea. When you call someone into your office that way, it's usually because you're giving them bad news—cutting their hours, or laying them off, or chewing them out for something."

Andrea nodded. "I agree. That's why it's so perfect. We're trying to win hearts and minds here. Most of the time, we deliver all the bad news behind closed doors. But when we start giving good news too, that's the day they start fearing us less and believing in us more. This is key to changing attitudes. We tell everyone we have an open-door policy, but when was the last time anyone came in to talk to you?"

Malik pondered that for a moment and replied, "You know, it hasn't been very often."

"That's because they fear us when they should trust us. We can't build trust if we don't talk to them. Get them talking. Get them coming to you with problems that you can fix for them. If they won't trust us, this radical delinking of the reviews and the raises will never work."

"I get it," Meghan said. "I was just thinking it would be kinda good to make sure everybody else heard about someone getting a raise."

Again Andrea smiled. "They will. You watch. Everybody talks. When you tap her on the shoulder and tell her to come to your office, every other employee within hearing distance will know it too. And most of them will think Sue's getting bad news. When she comes back out of your office smiling, everyone will want to know what happened. And the next thing that'll happen is magic."

"What?" both Malik and Meghan asked at the same time.

"I read case histories and I believe it. It's pure magic. I believe Sue will tell them, in her own words, one employee to another, with no management spin put on it. That is way more powerful than *you* telling people that you gave out a raise. The next time you call someone into your office, instead of trembling all the way in, they'll find themselves hopeful and, yes, still just a bit fearful. Sometimes, we will have to deliver bad news. But I'm convinced, after a few weeks of this, you'll have people coming up to you and asking, 'How come I never get called in for a raise?'"

Malik's eyes went wide. "Oh boy, how do I answer that question?"

Again Andrea beamed back at them. "It's a wonderful question, Malik. You invite them in on the spot and then you tell them the truth. And when you do that, don't sugarcoat anything. They asked, now you tell them. Again, though, you don't critique. You coach. You'd say something like, 'John, we're trying as a team to increase our production levels. When you can show me you are doing things to help the team, when you can show improvement over where you are today by, you know, moving the units down the line faster and stuff, then we'll be talking raise. Just bring your game up and keep it up. Can you do that?' And then if he says yes, you're done. If he says he doesn't know how, now you go into coach mode and you show him. And every employee that you've tried to train better before, that tuned you out and didn't follow directions, well, suddenly you're the guy who's going to help them make more money, and this time they'll listen."

Malik scratched his head, and Andrea could see another question coming.

"So, we just go down our list of people, identify the ones to get raises, and call them into the office and give them the raise. And we don't talk to the others unless they come to us?"

"Oh, good question, Malik," Meghan chipped in.

Now it was Andrea's turn to scratch her head. "Let me think. You know I read all about this but I'm still learning too. So…no, no, I think it gets weird then. I mean you don't want to give the impression that everybody you ask to come to your office gets a raise. I suggest…" Andrea paused as she collected her thoughts. Malik and Meghan sat quietly, nearly holding their breath.

Looking like she was more certain now, Andrea continued, "I suggest you simply go right down the list, alphabetically, and call each of them in one at a time. Let's see, you've each got thirty people, so I'd say you have time to do two to three meetings every day and you can finish by the end of the month.

"Meghan, you'll start with Sue and give her a raise as we discussed. Then you do the second person on the list, and if he or she isn't really ready for a bump up, you tell them what they need to improve on and be specific and say you'll be watching, and when you see improvement, they'll start making more money. Remember, we aren't critiquing. We're coaching. We're helping them identify specifically what they have to do to make more money."

Malik grimaced a bit. "Seems awkward, Andrea. I mean, some will get raises and the others get a big no. Seems like a really negative thing to do."

Andrea thought for a moment and replied, "I get your point. I think, though, you can make it more upbeat. Remember, most of these folks are not expecting a raise anyway. So this is what I'd do. Who's the first one on your—oh yeah, Mike Albers. Call him in and say something like, 'Mike, I just wanted to tell you that you are doing really well at'— you know, x, y, and z. Figure out something that they are doing well and lead off with a thank-you to them for the good effort. Then follow that with 'and I just want to make sure we're on the same page. The real issue you need to find an answer to is your arrival time. It hurts us in the morning when we are short a body for the first twenty minutes. And now with the bonus program being a shared goal for everyone, it's even more important. I'm just telling you that you're a good worker when you're here, but you need to find a carpool or an earlier bus or something. That's all that's standing between you and a raise. Think you can do that?' Always put it right to them. You're asking them point blank: can you solve this? Make sense?"

Malik nodded his head.

Meghan jumped in, "OK, that helps me too. So, I thank them first—and boy, we don't do enough of that—then I tell them what I think they're doing well. Next, I refer to the one thing they need to improve on and tell them when they do, they'll see a raise coming. Then ask them right up front if they can do it. Kind of a formula, right?"

"What if they have lots of things they could improve on?" Malik asked.

Andrea nodded. "I know some of them do. But for this, zero in on the most important thing and only address one weak point at a time. You might even say something like, 'We all have things we can be better at and most of us have more than one, but this is what is the most important to the team right now. After you beat that problem and get a raise, we can see what other opportunities there are.' Sound OK to you?"

As Malik nodded his head, Meghan asked the next logical question. "What about the other thing? I'm supposed to thank them and tell what they are doing well. What if they aren't doing anything well?"

"First of all, I'm willing to bet that you'll be able to think of something. Maybe, like Sue, they're really friendly or funny and they keep their coworkers in a good mood. If you think about it and they really have nothing they're good at, then you have a different kind of problem. Why are they still collecting a paycheck? You must have seen something good or you would've booted them by now. But no matter what, giving good news or bad, we have to tell the truth. We don't help anybody by shining them on. Tell it like it is, but give them a specific goal and see how they tackle one aspect of their job at a time. OK?"

There was a period of silence in the room as everyone considered what they'd just discussed.

Finally, Andrea said, "So, if there are no other questions, finish looking over the list of people on your form and make notes on all your decisions. Bring them back to me by five o'clock tomorrow. I'll look through them over the weekend, and we'll start doling out the raises and chatting with the others next week. Meghan, why don't you do Sue's raise tomorrow so people will hear about it before the weekend?"

Tentatively, Meghan nodded, and the two supervisors shared a worried glance. As the clock struck five, the three of them left the room.

Andrea started tidying up her desk and checked her To-Do list to see what was scheduled for tomorrow.

A soft knock on the door caused her to look up. Standing there were three line workers, two she recognized and one she didn't.

Paula Mathers, a Line 3 worker, spoke up. "Ms. Lane, is it OK if we come in and talk for a minute?"

Andrea nodded and pointed to an extra chair in the corner. "Absolutely, pull up one more chair and join me. I'm sorry, I don't remember names as well as I used to. Paula, I know you, and Farley, we've talked a few times, but I—"

"Ted. Ted Brunson," the third visitor said. "I'm on Line 5 in the Inspection role."

"Of course, Ted, thank you. So, tell me, what can I do for the three of you?"

Paula eyed the other two, then began, "Ms. Lane, we understand that sometimes changes are made, but we are, well, very unhappy about having our base pay cut ten percent."

Fighting the urge to defend herself instantly, she said, "Tell me what you're thinking."

"Ma'am," Farley jumped in, "it kinda shook me up. I mean, I feel like I worked really hard to get those last two raises and now, in one afternoon, you just decided to take them away. It kinda makes me nervous about what else you can take away."

Ted spoke up, saying, "Me too. It doesn't seem right. And now you're changing the raise method too. Makes me think maybe Stan was right. This is a money grab. I feel like getting a raise now will not mean as much if you can just wipe it out and start some new program."

Andrea said nothing, trying to give them the time to say all they wanted.

The two men explained their feelings about the change for another ten minutes as Andrea took notes on what they were saying.

When they finished, Paula picked up where they left off. "You should know, there's a whole lot of others who feel as we do, and they aren't happy. Most of them didn't want to make you mad so they didn't want to come up here with us. But they want us to report back to them what you said."

Andrea let loose a soft sigh that she regretted doing instantly. Then, looking Paula in the eyes, she said, "I get it. I knew going in that this would be very scary for folks and I was wary of doing it. My goal, however, is to create a way that every employee in this department can share in the upside. If you've been around here for any length of time, you know that one supervisor after another has been pushing everyone to speed up and be more productive, right?"

Farley rolled his eyes, and all three of them nodded. Paula added, "Charlie is famous for it. He pushes us hard and tells us to speed up, but when we ask how we could do it faster, he says, 'Figure it out.' The company just wants us to work harder. It's always been that way."

"I know," Andrea said. "I worked down there too, remember. I'm just saying that all these years they urged you to work harder, but when you did, you didn't get a little extra piece of the pie. So I tried to change it to a system where you *would* get a piece of the action."

Ted shook his head. "But why did you take ten percent away first? Couldn't you have left it all with us and just given us a bonus on top of our base pay?"

"Ted, it's an excellent question. And the answer is yes, I could've, but it wouldn't have worked." Andrea said it and paused for what she knew would come next.

All three of them asked it at the same time. "Why?"

"Look, I've worked for companies before that put in a bonus program and virtually every one failed. There are all kinds of ways to structure a bonus but, generally speaking, almost everyone gets it wrong. I read a lot about it, and studies have shown that the bonus amount has to be high enough to motivate people. And long story short, if I just added it on, it wouldn't have been enough to motivate you."

"It would motivate me," Paula said. "I'd like to make anything more than what I make now."

"Suppose the bonus was fifteen dollars. Would that have you stoked all month long and make you focus on working harder?"

"Fifteen dollars?" Paula asked. "I thought you said it could be considerably more."

"It can only be that much if we claw part of it out of the base pay and—"

"All you're doing is giving us back what used to be ours anyway," Farley said.

"In a way I am," Andrea replied. "But by structuring it this way, I'm getting you to focus on it. I'm getting everybody to focus on it, and that's what was missing before when one supervisor after another implored you to speed up. See, what we're really doing here is saying that every extra item you produce over and above the normal average adds profit for the company. So we're taking part of that profit and sharing it with you. Now, we make a little less in profit, but it's money we would never have if you didn't work harder."

"It still doesn't seem fair," Ted said. "I mean, did you lower your own pay by ten percent?"

Andrea wasn't prepared for that question. After considering her options, she told the truth. "No, I didn't. But I'm not participating in the bonus either."

The three of them sat quietly for a moment until Farley spoke up. "So, Ms. Lane, I guess that's why it just doesn't seem fair to take our ten percent away."

"I get it," Andrea said. "So I'm going to ask you to trust me. See, for the last six years, we have averaged almost exactly the same amount of production. We've failed to improve on that in any way. So I set the goal for the month at one twelfth of the average yearly production expecting that you won't have any problem making back your original base wage. But by doing that, the math adds up faster, and now if you merely do what you've always done, you make the same amount of money but it's paid to you for different reasons. If you exceed the goal, you basically give yourself a bonus every month, making your overall pay higher than it was before. The company wins, the customer wins, and the employee wins."

The room grew silent as the employees tried to grasp all that Andrea was saying. Finally, Ted asked, "Can you guarantee we'll make more?"

"I have no power to guarantee anything, Ted. However, I did my research and it turns out that the crew made within five percent of the average in twenty-three out of the last twenty-four months. The odds are extremely good that you'll make it every time anyway."

Paula tilted her head and asked, "Well, then why take it away in the first place?"

"Because I need everyone to focus on it and do their best every day so we don't fall short. And by structuring the bonus this way, I believe we *decrease* the chance we might have a month with a shortfall and *increase* the odds that you'll do more and make more in the bonus. I believe this will work, and for what it's worth, if I'm wrong about that, I'll lose my job and this experiment will end. You'll get your ten percent back but have no opportunity to increase your earnings with a bonus."

The three said nothing for a few seconds until Ted said, "We still have the pay raise issue. That doesn't seem fair either."

"Ted, let me ask you this: have you peaked?" Andrea asked.

"What do you mean?"

"Have you peaked? Are you already as good as you ever can be at your job?"

Ted glanced at Farley and Paula and replied, "Well, no. I mean, I think I get a little better every day."

"I agree. And I think all your teammates on the lines have the potential to constantly improve. The new raise plan gives the supervisors a chance to reward employees for incremental improvement on a much more frequent basis. Why should you have to wait a year for a reward? If you're doing well, you should get it right away."

"I didn't think of it that way," Ted said. "I ain't never heard of any other company doing it this new way."

"The world is changing. We're just trying to develop ways to keep up with it," Andrea said. "You tell the others that I'll talk to anybody who wants to come and discuss it with me. I can't tell you how impressed I am that you three had the courage to confront the issue. We need more people thinking for themselves and discussing how we can make this a better company for everyone."

Continuing, Andrea said, "So go back and tell everyone that I'm dedicated to doing whatever it takes to make this a success that they will value and appreciate. I don't want a single person to make less than they were making before. I want you all to have a chance to share in the company's financial success, and the only way I can think of doing that is to restructure compensation so that part of your pay is for showing up and part of it is for performance. If I'm wrong, I'll figure out a way to make it up to all of you."

Paula looked at her two compatriots, then back to Andrea. "We were hoping you'd give us our ten percent back again. That's what everybody wanted to hear."

"I know," Andrea replied quietly.

She continued, "I'm asking you to trust me even though I know that management has not always given you much reason to do that. I...I appreciate that you came up and talked to me like you did. That took guts."

After a short pause, Paula said, "Well, we've taken enough of your time. Thank you for seeing us."

The three rose from their seats and headed to the door.

As they departed, Andrea called out, "Guys. I'll talk to you or anyone else anytime. Remember, I was on the lines just two years ago. I'm still that same person. Being a VP didn't somehow magically make me different. I remember what I cared about back then and I won't allow myself to betray your trust or do anything I think would harm you. Thank you for coming to see me so we could talk."

The three nodded back to her. Ted mumbled something that resembled a "we'll see." They walked down the stairs to the manufacturing floor as Andrea sat at her desk and put her head in her hands.

Pressure's on now, Andi. Now, I gotta do it.

FRIDAY, FEBRUARY 9

Charlie Jensen had been in her office for only six minutes, but he was ready to leave five minutes ago. Andrea had not been happy with him and had made her points very clear as she discussed his no-notice exit on Thursday. Missing the meeting had meant that Andrea would have to go over the entire concept of the new raise system again, wasting valuable time.

Andrea gave him a sheet of paper printed from the Excel program and walked him through the plan. She explained step-by-step how to evaluate the employees and make decisions on raises. During that time, Charlie said nothing.

Stopping for a breath of air, Andrea said, "So, that's it. That's how we're going to do reviews and raises from now on. What questions do you have?"

Charlie looked at the Vice President and shook his head. "Are you kidding me? This is a crock. This will never work!"

Patiently, having expected nothing less from Charlie, Andrea replied, "Tell me why."

"Well, first of all," Charlie began, "I ain't never heard of anything like this. We're a big company and all big companies do stuff the same way. And second of all, I got three employees on this list who are expecting their yearly review and yearly raise this month—any day now, in fact. If they don't get it, there's gonna be hell to pay."

"That's it? That's all you've got?" Andrea retorted.

Surprised by Andrea's lack of concern, he muttered, "No. No, there, um, there's lots of things."

"Name another," Andrea ordered.

"Well, it's stupid. I don't want to have to keep calling people into my office and saying, um, you're doing a good job with the stickers so I'm giving you a twenty-cent raise. That...that's just dumb."

"Charlie, you know what our competitive position is. If we don't start increasing productivity and getting people to care more about quality, our competitors are going to eat our lunch. Then..." Andrea hesitated as she decided to pick her words carefully. "Then there will be layoffs. Maybe lots more than we think. A slew of your workers on Lines 3 and 4 may find themselves out of work. We need to make changes now. Can I count on you to be a team player and follow the plan?"

"Howie never would've done this. Now he's gone and you got promoted and you're just temporary. You can't make all these changes stick. I've been around here for thirty years. I know what's what. I don't like this. I'll have me a chat with Bentley and that'll be the end of it."

Andrea shook her head. "Mr. Bentley is in New York with the CFO. He'll be back by mid next week. I want to get going on this now. I need your answer."

Charlie's face grew red and he rose from his seat. "You're moving too fast. I got too much to think about. Let me have the weekend to think on it and I'll give you my answer on Monday."

Without waiting for Andrea's reply, he bolted for the door and left the room.

Andrea dropped her head into her hands and pressed her eyes closed.

Robbie was walking down the hall as Charlie bolted out. He stopped at Andrea's door and peered in. Seeing her with her head in her hands, he said, "It went that well, huh?"

Andrea looked up and smiled weakly. "If I, you know, like strangled Charlie, would I get into any trouble?"

"I guess that answers my question," Robbie said. "I hate to follow that up with more bad news, but…"

"But what?"

"Um, I have more bad news," Robbie said.

"Lay it on me," Andrea mumbled.

"Two of my key guys in the warehouse quit today. No notice. Got better paying jobs. I'll be short-handed for a while."

Andrea breathed a sigh of relief, then followed with an apology. "Sorry, I was expecting something that affected manufacturing. I mean, I'm sorry for you. You don't need that right now."

"Well, actually," Robbie said, "it *does* affect you. We're already starting to run behind on getting the shipments out. Your bonus program is based on number of units completed, but the bank doesn't count them as completed until they are shipped. If you don't do the same thing, you can't report your numbers to the bank or anyone else because they won't match the official report."

Andrea stared off into space for a moment, then asked, "But don't you always get everything shipped out same day?"

"We used to, but we never guaranteed it. Now, with Julio and Carl leaving, we're going to run way slower. Even if I hired somebody tomorrow—which isn't likely, by the way—we'll already have a backlog to work through. Last time I hired for that position, it took me nearly two weeks. If that happens again, we could have a record low month."

Again, Andrea pressed her eyes closed as she leaned back in her chair. The room was silent as Robbie gave her time to wrap her head around it.

Finally, Robbie said, "This is where you say, 'Oh shit!'"

Andrea chuckled quietly to herself and muttered, "Oh shit." A second later she followed that up with a rhetorical question. "What else can go wrong?"

Robbie gave her a "you shouldn't say that out loud" look.

Seeing the look on his face, Andrea blurted out, "Oh, God, you're right. Did I say that out loud? I should know better!"

Too late. Heavy and rapid footsteps could be heard running down the hall.

Malik arrived at her door and called out, "Andrea, Line 2 is down. The whole thing shuddered and then stopped. The mechanic is off today. What do we do?"

Line 2 was down for three hours before the backup repair service got it up and running. Today's output would be far short of the goal. In fact, the entire Manufacturing Division was now sixteen percent below the total goal through the ninth of the month. Andrea stared at the production numbers through February and found herself fighting off the urge to panic. She tried to set her fears aside and headed out to the floor to see what they could do without Line 2.

Forty minutes later, back in the office, Meghan showed up at her door. "Andrea, have you got a minute?"

Putting her notes aside, Andrea flashed her most reassuring smile and said, "Of course. What can I do for you?"

Meghan entered, closed the door behind her, and sat down opposite her boss. "I'm having a bit of a problem. I feel like I get what I'm supposed to do with this new review and raise system, but I did as you said—tapped Sue on the shoulder and asked her to come to my office at the next break. Just like you said, nearly everybody near her overheard and shot her a fearful look."

"OK, um, so where's the problem?"

"Well, now that I'm about to do it, I'm not sure exactly what I'm supposed to say. I guess I need a…a quick refresher or something."

Andrea nodded. "I get it. It is sort of daunting to do something like this for the first time. Fact is, I haven't done it either, but I've read a lot about it and I feel confident I could do it."

Meghan stared at her as she waited for some guidance.

Finally, Andrea said, "Tell you what. Pretend you're Sue and I'll be you telling her about the raise. This is how I think it should go."

Meghan nodded eagerly, realizing this is exactly what she needed—specifics, not generalities.

Andrea thought for a moment, then began, "Sue, I know this is your break, so I won't take long. I just wanted to tell you that I'm happy you are working with us and I believe you are a real asset to the company. You have a very cool ability to make your coworkers' days go better, just by being yourself. And every day I see improvement in the quality of your work.

"As you know, in our new system we aren't doing formal reviews or yearly raises anymore; we're rewarding workers as they deserve it instead. You've only been with us a little more than six months, but we feel you are very deserving of a raise right now. Effective retroactively back to February first, we're raising your hourly rate by sixty cents, which is about a hundred extra dollars per month for you."

Andrea paused, giving Meghan time to finish her notes, then continued, "Then stop and let her respond. Hopefully she'll be happy, and the rest is easy. But if she comes back and says something like, 'People told me to expect something closer to a dollar raise,' then you follow that up with saying this: 'Bear in mind that with the new system, raises are given out as your work effort, your value to the company, and your attitude about being here continue to improve or have a positive impact. At the rate you are going, I fully expect you'll see more raises this year that will put you over that target. Also, remember, there is no limit to how fast, how much, or how often you can get a raise. I'm hoping this is likely the first of many.'"

Andrea stopped talking and gazed at Meghan. She was furiously writing notes down.

"Meghan, don't try to memorize this. It was just an example. You should just speak from the heart, and I'm guessing it will come out something like what I said."

Meghan nodded her agreement and breathed deeply. "That helps me a lot. I see what you did. First you told her it wouldn't take long, which could actually be interpreted as good *or* bad news. But then you immediately put her at ease by telling her how happy you are with her work. You gave some examples of what she was doing right, and you reminded her how the new review and raise system works. You didn't waste any time. You just told her how much she was getting and you translated it into dollars per month. I like that. Sometimes cents per hour doesn't sound so great."

"Exactly," a pleased Andrea said. "So put her at ease, compliment her, give specifics, remind her about the system, and tell her what she gets. It only takes a minute or so, then you can answer her questions."

Meghan beamed. "Right. I can do that. I...I just wasn't sure what to say. And I pictured it taking longer too."

She rose from her chair and said, "Thanks, Andrea. I feel better now. I better get out there. The break starts in a few minutes."

As Meghan reached the door, Andrea called out to her supervisor. "Meg, remember, if she asks questions you don't know the answer to, be humble. Simply say, 'This is all new to me too. I don't know, but I'll find out and have an answer for you quickly.' And one other thing."

"What?"

Andrea smiled at her star supervisor and said, "Come and tell me how it went. I'm excited to see this system in action."

SATURDAY, FEBRUARY 10

Precisely at nine o'clock, Andrea tested the front door to the Professor's Bar and Grill and found that Tyler had unlocked it already.

He was seated, reading the sports section of the newspaper and sipping coffee already.

"You know you can get all that and more online, don't you?"

Tyler looked up and said, "Good morning to you, too. I still love to read the newspaper. I'm old school, sue me."

"I'll do better than that: I'll pay you. I'm sure I can't afford your usual consulting rate, but how about I pay you with a box of chocolate-covered cherries?"

"Sold!" Tyler exclaimed. "You know my weakness and now you're exploiting it. Have you no shame?"

Andrea shook her head. "After this week, I have no pride or self-confidence either."

Tyler laughed. "I only do business consulting. For the rest of that stuff, you have to see a shrink."

He rose from his seat and went to the backside of the bar to retrieve two plates of breakfast staying warm in the oven. Holding them up, he said, "I thought we'd do something different this morning. A little bacon and eggs and, you know, other high cholesterol stuff."

"Bring it on. I'm ready for anything," Andrea said, chuckling.

They both dug into their meal and got through three mouthfuls before Tyler said, "OK, I love this part. I get to eat while you talk. Tell me about the week."

Andrea gave him the rundown on the cold reception her new raise and review plan received. She told him about the meeting with Malik and Meghan and how Charlie missed the meeting and was already fighting her on the changes. She explained the interdepartmental problem she was having with Logistics and the backlog of orders they expected due to inadequate staffing in the shipping department. Finally she got to the one piece of news she was looking forward to telling her uncle.

"Lest you think I am a total screw up, I do have some good news."

"Good news, what's that?" Tyler deadpanned.

"It's what happens when something actually works like it's supposed to. Unc, it was so wonderful to hear from Meghan. She gave her first raise out to a fairly new worker named Sue, who works on Line 5 and is doing really well. She's only been with us six months, so she didn't expect a raise.

"I told Meg to call her into her office and tell her what she is doing well and give her a sixty-cent-per-hour raise." As Andrea finished the sentence, she found she couldn't stop herself from beaming.

"Must've gone well," Tyler guessed.

"It didn't go *well*; it went *spectacularly*. Sue was nervous and a bit scared when she came into Meghan's office, but within seconds she was overwhelmed. It really *was* magic. Suddenly her boss was telling her how pleased she was with her work and that she was getting a raise retroactive to February first. Meg said she was almost giddy and started crying. She had no questions, no expectations, very little pre-meeting angst and she was happy that someone recognized how hard she was working.

"Meghan was ecstatic about it. She watched from her office as Sue went back out to the line and started telling all her coworkers. She got hugs and Meg said she had a smile on her face for the rest of the day. I'm telling you, if people will just give us a chance and some time to make all this happen, they'll love this system. Knowing they could get a raise any day, I think they'll give their best on every shift."

Tyler chewed off the end of a bacon slice and smiled back at her. "I'm glad for you. It feels pretty good when something goes right, doesn't it?"

"You know it," Andrea agreed.

"So, not to ruin the moment," Tyler said, shifting gears, "but what are you going to do about Charlie?"

Andrea rolled her eyes. "I don't know. He was one of Bentley's first hires and he's been there longer than dirt, but honestly, he does next to nothing and he's been getting away with it for so long that he thinks it's just fine. When I gave him his review, it was the first time he hadn't got a raise since he started there. So he kinda hates me anyway. I think he's waiting for me to get fired."

They ate together in silence for a few moments, then Tyler dropped a heavy reminder on her. "You have forty-nine days left to turn your department around. A company that survives in this new world, with the pace of change happening so fast, has to have everyone pulling together, truly working as a team. Can you do that if Charlie is rowing in the other direction?"

Andrea said nothing, but the look on her face told Tyler she knew what she had to do. "Problem is, he'll just go running to Bentley to overrule me."

"Yup, he will. But, Andi, you're forgetting one little thing."

"What's that?"

"You have a contract with Bentley. He gave you two months. If he tries to overrule you, wave that piece of paper in his face and remind him he essentially gave you *carte blanche* to do what had to be done. If he overrules you, he negates the contract. Let him know in no uncertain terms that you would fight that."

"I would?" Andrea asked.

"Yes, you would," Tyler replied.

"Because…because I'm in the right and I would win?"

Tyler shook his head. "No, you'd probably lose. But when the bank finds out that your contract was violated, Juggernaut would lose too. Bankers don't like doing deals with pikers."

"Hmmm," Andrea hummed. "Never thought of it that way. By the way, that was a delicious breakfast. I can feel my arteries clogging already."

Tyler laughed. "Yeah, go ahead and make jokes. You've earned it. But before you leave, I want to remind you of one more thing."

"I'm listening.

Tyler finished off his coffee and said, "Remember, in this fast-paced world, the companies that succeed in a big way have to build agility and swift but careful action into everything they do. That means the employees need to be on board and they have to be able to participate and make things happen as needed, not just when management says they can do it. They have to be able to respond quickly to outside threats, competitors, changes in the market-place, and anything else that gets between them and their goals. That means they have to be educated and taught how to think for themselves and still keep all the corporate objectives in mind."

"That's, um, that's a lot," Andrea said.

"It is. But nothing less than that will actually work long term. You are trying to build a fast-paced business in which everyone has a stake in success and knows that they have the power to make a difference. So when you truly understand that, tell me, how would you describe that company? One word, Andi. What would it be?"

"One word?" Andrea asked.

Tyler nodded. "Think about it."

Andrea savored her last swig of coffee and retreated into herself to think. She knew that her uncle was a big believer in succinctness and this was often how he had tested his students. She mulled it over, then locked eyes with him and said, "Nimble?"

Tyler smiled. "That works. Just remember your old nursery rhymes—you know, with a little modification: Exec be nimble, Exec be quick."

MONDAY, FEBRUARY 12

At 8:15, Charlie Jensen entered Andrea's office with a smug look on his face. Without being invited to sit down, he made himself at home in the chair directly in front of Andrea's desk. Andrea looked up from her paperwork, peering over her reading glasses.

"I appreciate you being here so early, Charlie. Did you have time to think some things over this weekend?"

"I did, and I've decided that I was right the first time. I don't like your idea of how to handle reviews and raises and I don't believe it will work. I'm also getting a lot of questions about the pay situation and what'll happen if we don't get production levels higher before the end of the month. I think the whole Manufacturing Department is just a few weeks away from crashing down."

Andrea stared back at him and replied, "You look like you'd be happy if that happened."

Charlie couldn't contain his smile. "I would. Bentley will fire you and I think he'll promote me to take your place."

Andrea calmly nodded. "So is this your way of telling me that you aren't going to participate in the new review and raises program?"

"Weren't you listening to what I said? Yeah, I won't do it. Got it?"

"I got it," Andrea acknowledged. "I just wanted to make sure I understood. So it looks like I will have to do your reviews and raises for you."

Chuckling now, Charlie said, "Go ahead. Knock yourself out."

Andrea signed a piece of paper in front of her and looked Charlie in the eyes. "The problem is that it has to get done, and if I do it, I have to ask myself, what do I need you for?" She handed the form over to Charlie and said, "I'm terminating your employment effective immediately. Take this to HR and they will process you out. I'll have security escort you out of the building after you pick up your personal belongings. Thank you for your service."

Charlie's eyes grew wide and he stammered, "Y-you can't do that! I have, um, I have seniority here! My lawyer will hear about this. My crew here will be totally pissed. I'll bend Bentley's ear about this and he'll reinstate me and fire you."

Andrea looked back at him and calmly said, "Knock yourself out."

An hour later, Andrea called Reese Donnelley into her office. As she waited for him to arrive, she flashed back to her Saturday morning breakfast with Uncle Tyler and was thankful she had followed his suggestion to move more quickly. When she got home that morning, she called Carol Womack, someone she knew and could trust, and confirmed her suspicion that no one on Line 3 or 4 would be unhappy if Charlie were suddenly not their boss anymore. After more discussion, she asked Carol if Sheldon, Charlie's favorite, would be an improvement over Charlie as the new supervisor. She could almost hear Carol rolling her eyes.

"Are you kidding? Shell is like a mini-me for Charlie. Carved out of the same block of lazy wood. Please, I beg you, don't put Shell in charge," Carol implored.

"Well, that seemed pretty clear," Andrea replied. "Any suggestions then?"

There was a pause on the other end of the line, then Carol said, "Well, Reese Donnelley is a good man and he's a hard worker. Doesn't say much but everyone respects him. He might be interested."

Andrea sat at her desk and replayed that conversation in her head. *I don't really know him. I guess we'll find out in a few minutes if he could do the job.*

Reese showed up at her door a few moments later. If he was worried about being called to the VPs office, he didn't show it.

Andrea greeted him at the door and shook his hand. Pointing to a chair, she said, "Reese, you've been with us for two years and I haven't had many opportunities to talk to you. I imagine you may have heard already about Charlie."

Wearing a championship poker face, he nodded and said, "Yes, ma'am, I did."

Andrea jumped in slowly. "I was wondering if you had any suggestions about who might be a good replacement for him."

Reese stared back at her with a million questions in his eyes, but he only asked one. "Why ask me?"

"Because I hear you do good work and people respect you. I wanted to hear what your thoughts on it were," Andrea countered.

Reese rubbed his chin and said, "Carol is sharp. And Lennie Rule, over on Line 5, is a hard charger. I know he's interested in moving up."

Andrea pretended to write those names down and said, "Carol and I go way back, and I know she's retiring before the end of the year. Lennie is a very good man, but all his experience is on Line 5, and 3 and 4 are very different processes, but I'll give them some thought."

Andrea paused for a moment, and Reese continued to calmly make himself comfortable in the chair. After a few seconds, she asked, "I was wondering if you have any suggestions about how we could improve the work flow on Lines 3 and 4?"

For just a second, Andrea thought she saw something in his demeanor that changed.

"Ma'am, I mind my own business most of the time, but I have a few opinions. I'm not sure you'd appreciate hearing them, though."

"But I would. Just between you and me, I'd like to hear some constructive criticism. Fire away."

Reese hesitated for a moment, then launched into it. "Well, I for one am glad Charlie's gone. Of course, it's kinda hard to tell. If he wasn't arriving late or leaving early, he was on an extended break or doing nothing at all. I've wondered what kind of company Juggernaut is to let a supervisor get away with that. So, I'd say, first of all, you need a replacement that works hard and sets a good example. Then you gotta make some changes. Sheldon, for example, should not be in the number one spot on Line 3. The first person on the line sets the pace for both the lines, and Shell, well, he cares about his job less than Charlie does…er, did. Put someone like Donovan Miller or Julie Sikes first and we could do a lot more. There are at least four people on both lines doing shoddy work, forcing us to have a higher percentage of product going to the fine-tuning pile. It's wasted effort, but no one in management ever spends any time retraining those folks."

Reese stopped for a moment to catch his breath, then continued for another five minutes describing things that needed to be changed on the two lines. As he was wrapping up, he added, "And I don't mean to be a complainer, but I don't think anybody really understands this new bonus program or raise system. They may nod their heads when you explain it, but after you're gone, they all look at each other and ask questions no one can answer."

"You don't like either program?" Andrea asked.

"Ma'am, I'm not sure I understand them either. I don't think—well, I've said enough."

Andrea shook her head. "Reese, I don't know about you, but I'm trying hard to fix some problems, and along the way, it wouldn't surprise me if I made some mistakes. All I want from anybody is the truth because I can't find my way without it. I need people to tell me the truth—even if it hurts. So, please, you haven't said enough. Finish your thought."

Reese cocked his head and said, "I ain't never worked for a company that really wanted the truth. Are you sure that's what you want?"

"Oh yes," Andrea said, smiling.

"Well, ma'am, I don't think you thought this out. I mean, launching the new bonus program in February—a short month—and giving us a tough goal to reach. Nearly insures that we won't make it. And everybody thinks that already, so they've practically given up on making extra money. And that makes it look like you're doing it just to cut costs. And then there's Sue. She got a raise, and from what I hear, she deserved it. That was good, but all the folks that were supposed to get their yearly raise this month, they're fuming. That's making it a downer for everybody else. I mean, I get what you're trying to do, but your execution of it is, well, too slow and off target."

Swallowing her pride and doing her best not to show how she felt hearing such a negative critique of her actions, she replied, "Those are all valid points, Reese. I appreciate you sharing them with me. I know I have to do better in a lot of ways. I have one other question for you."

Reese nodded and remained silent.

Struggling with the right way to word her question, Andrea started out slowly. "If I were to offer you a chance to help me make this a better place to work for everyone, would you accept the job of supervisor of Lines 3 and 4?"

Reese blinked. "You're offering me the job after what I just said?"

"No," Andrea said. "I'm offering you the job *because* of what you said."

Reese stared back at her and said, "I've never been a manager. I'll probably make mistakes."

Andrea smiled. "Then we can both belong to the same club. Please accept. I think you'd do very well."

"Yes, ma'am. I accept!"

This time, Andrea grinned. "Well, let's you and me go out there and introduce the new supervisor to everyone. You can start today."

WEDNESDAY, FEBRUARY 14

By eight fifteen, Andrea was seated across from Mr. Bentley, alone in his office. It hadn't taken him long to call her in as soon as he arrived to start his day.

"I get back from New York and find out that, behind my back, you fired Charlie Jessup!"

"Jensen," Andrea corrected, then immediately wished she hadn't.

"What?" Bentley asked.

"I'm sorry, maybe I heard you wrong. His last name is Jensen. I, um, I thought I heard something different."

"Whatever!" Bentley bellowed. "He's been with me a long time and I didn't want you to fire him."

Andrea looked down at the carpet for a second as she carefully formulated her answer. "Sir, I am the VP of Manufacturing and he is in my department. VPs have always had authority to terminate employees. My job—all of our jobs—is to turn this company around in less than six months. Sometimes it can't be done without weeding out the underperformers."

"Charlie is a good guy. I know. I hired him, I think. And I see him in the hall every day and he always has a big smile."

"Sir," Andrea began again, "he doesn't do anything. He shows up late for work, he takes long breaks, and he leaves early every chance he gets. When he is here, he is shooting the breeze with some coworkers. He hands out full raises to people who also did

72

next to nothing to deserve them, and he is paid way too much money for the return we get."

Bentley rose from his chair behind his desk and said, "Doesn't matter. I made my decision. Reinstate him immediately."

"I can't do that," Andrea said.

"I just ordered you to."

"I know, but we have a contract, remember? You gave me two months to make the changes I wanted to try and in return I agreed to take a fifty percent pay cut and resign if you're not happy with those changes. We have a deal and it's signed by both of us. Implicit in the language of the deal is that I will have the right to do what I have to do. If you rescind my decisions, you also rescind the contract."

"So?" Bentley countered.

"So, if you rescind the contract, then I will resign, and before I leave I'll tell the bank what happened and they will know that you got rid of me because I was making improvements."

"You...you trying to blackmail me or something?" Bentley asked, his eyes growing wide as he spoke.

"Not at all. I'm trying to save you and the company. I'm taking action, which is not only what you wanted, but it's also what you ordered. You should know, by the way, that I appointed Reese Donnelly as the new supervisor of Lines 3 and 4 and it has been a very popular move. No one liked Charlie. Reese has already done more in two days than Charlie did all last year. And he does it for less too."

Bentley sat back down. "Less? How much less?"

"Charlie was getting $135,000 per year. Reese is—"

"He's what! No way! We weren't paying him that much," Bentley nearly yelled it as he cut her off.

"Your former VP of Manufacturing, Howard, gave him a monster amount of overtime and the maximum raise every year for the last fifteen years. Charlie made way more than I do. Reese, on the other hand, was given a hefty raise from his hourly pay and he now makes sixty-five thousand. I just saved the company seventy thousand dollars this year."

Bentley spun his chair around to face out the window. He sat there quietly as Andrea decided she didn't need to say any more.

Finally, after what seemed like hours but was only a fraction of that, Bentley turned to her and asked, "Well, what are you waiting for? Don't you have some work to do?"

Andrea rose from her seat, but feeling uncertain about the end result, she asked, "So we still have a deal, right?"

"Yes, yes, get to work," Bentley said as he gave her a flap of the back of his hand, as though he were shooing a fly.

Andrea did her best to suppress a smile and exited quickly.

FRIDAY, FEBRUARY 16

The next few days of the week were a whirlwind. Andrea spent a few hours coaching Reese on the best ways to interact with his employees and found him to be a natural. As a quiet man, he found it easy to listen more than talk, and being a good listener, he learned far more than he expected about Charlie's demotivating style and about every employee's concerns and wishes. Acting on them, he began immediately to have the raise discussion with the remaining workers who expected a full review and a raise in February.

Meghan and Malik saw the flurry of activity that Reese generated and they sped up their reviews and raises to the February anniversary employees as well. More than anything, Reese encouraged people to speak their piece, and he actually took immediate action to resolve their concern. Nearly the moment that the Line 3 and 4 workers sensed that management would *actually* respond, the morale and the productivity began to rise. Coupled with the personnel position changes Reese made on the line, the two middle lines began to outpace the others.

Being Friday night, Andrea sent out a text invitation to the other five VPs about meeting at Brannigan's and comparing notes over a drink. Gretchen, Sammi, and Rob texted back affirmatively within minutes. Craig and Tim said they had other commitments.

As Andrea was preparing to leave, Stan Heller, the worker who yelled at Andrea from Line 5 during her presentation about the review process, stormed into her office.

Practically frothing at the mouth, he screamed out, "I was right. These new deals are only being done to screw us out of our money! Meghan called me in today and told me I was getting a four-percent raise. That's like nothing. Less than a dollar an hour. I've always gotten the max raise before, and I need it again. This is absolute bullshit, and I'm not standing for it!"

"Stan, take a seat," Andrea began. "Let's talk about how this works again." Reluctantly, Stan sat down and frowned back at Andrea. "I'm sure Meghan explained that you are likely to see other raises during the year as you work on those things you and she agreed you could improve on?"

"I'm doing great already. I'm not gonna get much better. What do you want from me?"

"Stan, I'm a VP and I still have a lot of opportunity for improvement—"

Stan stood up. "No shit! You're screwing everything up. You're the one who fired Charlie and he was a good guy."

"I was about to say that I can improve and so can every employee here. You included. And the difference between what we used to do and what we are doing now is that when you improve, management will notice and you'll be financially rewarded for it. Are you telling me that you're already perfect, Stan?"

Stan looked away. "I just don't like the new deal. I like to know how much I'm making."

"Do you like knowing that no matter what you do, you can't get another raise until next March? How is that better than telling you there is no limit to how much you can earn if you improve your value to the company?"

"I'm still not buying into it," Stan said defensively.

Andrea considered the wide range of responses she could make and decided it was best to agree to disagree. "I understand. I appreciate that you took the time to tell me how you feel. I like that you speak from the heart and say exactly what you think, so now I'm going to do the same thing."

Stan looked up at her, and for a brief moment, Andrea was sure she saw fear in his eyes.

She continued, "I'm going to do my best to change your mind. I don't like it much when a good, steady, competent employee thinks I'm trying to pull a fast one. I'm hoping that maybe you'll give me a chance to prove myself to you. Will you give me a few months to change your mind, Stan?"

He started to say something, but stopped himself. Then, in a low voice, he muttered, "Well, I-I'm not going anywhere."

Sensing that was as much of a victory as she was going to get, Andrea stood up and extended her hand to him. He eyed her, somewhat surprised by her reaction to his diatribe, and gave her an ever-so-brief shake.

As he walked out of her office, she called to him, "Good night, Stan. Have a good weekend." She forced herself to smile as she said it, believing as many do that a smile can be heard as well as seen.

When his footsteps quit echoing down the hall, she rose and closed her office door. She sat down again at her desk and tried to compose herself. After a few minutes, she did her best to shake it off and head down to Brannigan's.

I wanted to fight back, to explain why I was making all these changes, but I know being defensive won't work. I have to let them say their piece and gain their trust first. Every book I've read says you can't begin to gain their trust if they are scared to talk to you. You can't bring them around if you argue every point with them. They have to get to the point where they want to come in and talk with me. They have to trust that I won't fire every person or go ballistic over every big or small slight that I feel. But, oh boy, that really sucked.

SATURDAY, FEBRUARY 17

Uncle Tyler and Andrea sat down again for breakfast and she brought him up to date on all the events of the week.

As they finished their meal, Tyler said, "Well, I think you did pretty well for yourself. You cut out the cancer that Charlie was. Bentley backed down when you waved the contract in his face. You hired a much better supervisor, and after you described your meeting with Stan, I would say you wisely showed remarkable restraint."

"Wisely, huh?" Andrea asked, cocking her head. "You don't think that was cowardly. Robbie and Sammi both did."

Tyler's eyes grew wide. "Did they say that to you?"

"They didn't need to. I can read between the lines. They both said they would've yelled back and thrown him out of their office. And believe me, I wanted to."

Tyler stared at his niece and slowly smiled a crooked smile.

"What?" Andrea asked.

"You, my dear, are turning into a rather astute student of human nature."

"I am?"

"You bet," Tyler said. He sipped the last of his coffee, then finished his thought. "First of all, every management act is easier if you approach it with humility. Those managers who think they can do no wrong box themselves right into a corner that, sooner or later, they can't get out of. It's far easier if you admit your faults and agree with those who criticize you. Learn from it because there is always a grain of truth in every critical comment. If you had gone defensive, you wouldn't have got him to come around."

"I don't think I *did* get him to come around," Andrea said.

"I do. He now knows that you are someone more like him. Imperfect. He knows too that he can come in and talk to you because he already said the worst he could and you listened to it, complimented him on his work ethic, promised to do better, shook his hand, and sent your new friend on his way with a wish for a nice weekend. Bingo! All the things you needed to do to start building the base of a trusting relationship."

Andrea chuckled. "You make it sound like I planned that all along."

"Andi, no, I know you didn't. You reacted to him, but you held your temper and set aside your hurt feelings, then you made and remade the decision to win him over by not allowing his anger to turn you against him."

"So…Unc, you think I did the right thing?"

"No. I know you did the right thing. Remember, you need everybody in the boat rowing in unison. You can't get that if you don't build their trust."

Andrea had been ready to head for the door, but she stalled a moment and said, "The thing is, I know I need their trust, but it seems hard to do, especially in a short period of time."

"I know," Tyler agreed. "But forget about the time constraint. You can't hurry it, even if you really need to. I was reading an article the other day in *Forbes*. A fellow named Kevin Kruse wrote about the four things that help to create a happy, motivated, and productive workforce. Communication comes first. Your instinct that the employees need to feel they can come and talk to you about anything is spot on. Then comes growth. They have to feel that they can rise up, make more money, learn new skills, and gain promotions and that your style of management will help them to grow. Recognition is the third one—if they do well and management doesn't notice, then they'll lose motivation to continue. So you have to find ways to recognize them and celebrate their accomplishments with everyone. Then, if you can do those three things well, trust is the likely byproduct. When they find themselves trusting that you will lead them well and that you have their best interests at heart, the trust will flow in your direction."

Andrea pondered all that for a moment and said, "Sounds like a lot."

"Yup," Tyler said as he carried the dirty dishes back to the kitchen.

TUESDAY, FEBRUARY 20

The printer spit out the latest production report and Andrea wasted no time grabbing it and settling down into her chair to study the numbers. It confirmed exactly what she was sure she knew already. They weren't going to make the February goal.

At the pace they were going, and at the pace that the shipping department was getting the product packed and handed off to the trucking companies, they would miss the minimum goal by forty shipments. With only six working days left in the month, making up the forty would be next to impossible.

At Juggernaut, Lines 1 and 2 took the printed orders and gathered the product and all the accessories it needed, prepping them for assembly. Lines 3 and 4 put them together, adding the Glimmer Stones and additional features. Lines 5 and 6 did quality control, cleaned and shined up the items, double-checked to make sure everything customers ordered was accounted for, and pre-packaged them together, taping the paperwork on the outside, before sending them to Logistics. Line 5 also dealt with exceptions and worked on the fine-tuning items—those that didn't pass the quality inspection and needed a bit more work. Normally that was one in every thirty, but lately the quality had slipped and the rejects had increased.

As Andrea stared at the report and saw the reject rate rising, she shook her head. *Rising reject rates are almost always a byproduct of a disengaged workforce. When the rank and file employees don't take pride in their work or care about the outcome, quality goes south. I've got to do something about that.*

She rose from her desk and strolled out onto the floor, stopping in the center to gaze at the whiteboard mounted on the wall. It showed the total number of items produced by the line in February frozen for the night at 1,993. She knew they should be at several hundred more by now if they were going to show an average month and gain the middle range bonus that would pay them more than they used to make. She pursed her lips and turned to the left, then purposely walked directly toward the fine-tuning staging area. Eleven different items sat there, waiting for caring hands to repair or improve what wasn't done right the first time. Andrea shook her head again and glanced at the exit.

We're not going to catch up wishing for it. We've got to find a way to pick up the pace in the last six days.

She set her purse and coat on a table and rolled up her sleeves. Mumbling to herself, she said, "Wasn't so long ago I was doing this every day. I bet I still remember how."

She pulled a stool over and sat down. Taking the patio table and chair set that was the oldest item there, she read the notes from the quality control associate and started in on the repair.

Tim and Craig sipped their drinks at Brannigan's.

Craig loosened his tie and looked at the CFO. "Did you and Bentley have any luck in New York?"

Tim shook his head. "You gotta know the answer to that. I tell you, there is only one thing worse than our numbers right now, and that is Bentley's presentation skills. It was a disaster. Did you expect something else?"

"No, I guess I was just hoping. This has been a sweet little gig for you and me. I'm really not ready for it to end."

"I know. You still have plenty of years left, but I'd like to just wrap it up without too much drama before I head out and start collecting my pension."

Craig chuckled and said, "Well, the drama will all be over soon. You can retire, and I'll have to find a new gig. Bentley is… well, hell, I guess I knew all along it was his old man who had all the smarts. He was a real businessman. Junior is just a caretaker. He doesn't really even understand the business."

Tim nodded. Then he raised his hand to get the waitress's attention and signaled for another round.

"I don't know what I'm going to do, Sammi," Gretchen lamented.

The two of them sat in Sammi's office and did their best to try and make each other feel better.

"The sales are holding steady," Gretchen said, "but seriously, Clay, Larry, and Renee are all B-minus sales reps. I practically have to close every deal for them. Donovan is doing great, as usual, but he's talking about his six-week vacation coming up on March 5th, and we'll be without him for all that time."

"Is this the trip on the cruise ship all around Europe?" Sammi asked.

"Yeah," Gretchen said, her eyes downcast. "I can't ask him to reschedule. He's been planning it for nearly three years and Bentley approved it two years ago. What am I supposed to tell him? When you get back we'll be, like, two months away from folding?"

"Uh, no, obviously you can't say that," the HR VP replied.

They sat through a moment of uneasy silence.

Sammi broke it, saying, "Maybe you can light a fire under the other three. I don't know. Maybe this wacky idea Andrea has could work for you too. Dangle a bigger prize in front of the sales reps and motivate them to sell harder."

Gretchen shook her head. "I don't know. First of all, everything I'm hearing is that it isn't popular and clearly isn't working yet. Besides, how would I do that? Bentley's not going to OK more payouts for the reps. He doesn't even like the current pay structure."

"Let's face it, Gretch. This puppy is probably toast. I don't know what else I can do, and you're probably right about Bentley's attitude toward paying more. This fight may be over already."

The last UPS truck left the dock loaded with everything Juggernaut could ship out. Robbie lowered the bay door and locked it down. Hands on his hips, he looked around the warehouse at the ever-growing number of items that remained behind. All were products ready to be packaged and shipped but his smaller crew ran out of time to prepare them.

Mumbling to himself, he said, "If Julio and Carl were still here, the floor would be cleared. I sure miss them."

He grabbed his jacket from his office and started to head out of the building. Before he left the warehouse, he stopped in his tracks and placed his coat on a box by the door. Checking his watch, he thought, *It's only five thirty. What am I racing out for? So I can go home alone and eat a TV dinner?*

He rolled his sleeves up, flipped the lights back on, and pulled an empty cardboard box from storage. Talking out loud to himself again, he said, "Let's see what kind of a dent I can put in this pile. Andrea's team is cranking them out faster now, and the least I can do is keep up with them."

FRIDAY, FEBRUARY 23

After too much soul-searching and agonizing, Andrea decided to make her next announcement. She knew she was going to have to eat some crow and admit her own errors, but she was now convinced it had to be done.

At 4:45, the supervisors blew their whistles and work on all the lines ceased. Andrea stood on the fifth step of the stairway and used her strong voice to call out to everyone.

"I hate to lose fifteen productive minutes, but I think it'll be worth it. After discussions with Malik, Meghan, Reese, and Stan, I've decided to make some changes to the February bonus program."

She paused for a second, and as she did, a voice from Line 1 yelled back, "Here it comes. Management is going to take something else away from us."

Andrea smiled and shook her head. "Actually, I can understand why you think that, but the changes I have in mind are geared to fixing some of my own mistakes. First of all, using our average month data makes February a particularly bad month to start with. Fewer work days in the month make it way too hard to reach the goals we set.

"As you can see on the big whiteboard, we now have 2,467 units produced so far this month, but that is far short of the average goal. We have three levels of goals: if we hit 3,400 units produced, everyone gets a $300 bonus, which generally is about the same as what you gave up in the ten-percent pay reduction. The other two goals of 3,650 and 4,000 are totally out of reach, and truth is, it'll be hard to make the bottom goal too.

"I've—"

Another voice from the crowd yelled out, "We all figured that out a long time ago. So everyone is getting nothing, right?"

"This is on me. I picked goals that were too high for a short month. So, since I broke it, now I'm going to fix it. I'm changing it. Malik, go ahead and write in the new goals and the new dollar payout."

Everyone watched as Malik climbed the ladder and erased the old numbers, filling in new ones. When he was done, the lowest level goal was set at 2,900. The middle goal was 3,050, and the top goal was 3,300. Payouts per person were $300, $400, and $600, respectively.

Andrea began again. "This change puts the lower and middle goals within reach by the end of the month. I apologize for making the targets too aggressive, but as soon as we add today's totals, we should have a very interesting last three days of the month next week.

"Before I let you leave tonight, I want to tell you how the March bonus will work. I've written it all out here on this one-page flyer that the supervisors are passing out now. The major difference is that this will be a daily bonus program instead of monthly. It will make every day meaningful and every unit produced will add money to the pot that will be shared at the end of the month, pro-rated based on hours worked. You'll notice also that we now have six levels, and the amount added to the pot rises when we hit each level."

The March Bonus Program

Using what we learned in February, we are making some changes to the format of the March bonus program. First of all, it's hard to stay focused every day for a month so this new bonus program is based on each day's performance. Every day, we count the number of units produced for shipment and as each one is completed, dollars are added to the 'pool' which all of the Manufacturing Department employees will share in. Shares will be based on your % of hours worked. We have 92 people in the department and if everyone worked 8 hours a day, you would each get $1/92^{nd}$ of the bonus pool. But since some work more or less hours, you will get a pro-rated amount based on the hours you worked compared to what everyone else worked. Overall, it will still end up being close to $1/92^{nd}$.

Our goal for the month is 3,960 units. But the dollars added to the bonus pool are based on the number of units you finish by five o'clock—that is, quality-inspection-passing units. Here is the way the daily bonus amount will be calculated:

Units shipped	$ added to the bonus pool for each unit
1-50	$10.00
51-100	$11.00
101-140	$12.00
141-160	$13.00
161-180	$14.00
Over 180	$15.00

Completing 3,960 would put the pool at $45,540. Every extra order after 180 per day adds $15.00 to the pool. If you work the average number of hours, your share of the bonus pool would be $495. And it could be much more. By the way, our all-time record for most units shipped in one month is 4,212. Let's get at it!

Andrea paused, giving them time to read it over. As a few minutes went by and no hecklers called out at her, she let loose a quiet sigh of relief.

"The supervisors and I are here to answer any questions you may have, but I just want to say that I think these new goals for February are far fairer to you and the new process for March will be much more interesting and rewarding. Thank you very much for listening and have a great weekend."

She walked down to the floor and mingled with everyone, answering questions and staying until the last employee had left.

Meghan and Malik waved their good-byes to her as Reese grabbed his coat from his office.

The newest supervisor pulled his coat on and walked over to Andrea. "These numbers are better. I know that must have been hard, but you scored a few points with people and they seemed to like it."

"It's not a great idea, generally speaking, to alter the goals midgame like this, but you made some good points about the short month and I felt I had to do something. You think they liked it?"

Reese nodded. "Yeah. Well, they liked the new numbers better, but the jury's still out about the whole bonus thing. I think they'll feel a bit better when they actually see a bonus on their check. Still, some healthy skepticism here, you know."

"I know. Believe me, I know."

Andrea returned to her office and sat down behind her desk. Drained by the day's events, she wanted to lay her head down and fall asleep, but she knew that wasn't an option. Not yet, at least. Taking a deep breath, she left her office and headed toward the reject pile.

Robbie taped up the top of the sturdy crate holding another Value Vase and looked over his work. Satisfied it would get the item to the destination safely, he sealed it up and took another look at the staging area.

Checking his watch, he saw it was going on quarter to nine. Talking to himself, he said, "I did eight tonight. Only four more to go, but I'm outa gas. I'll come back tomorrow and catch us up so we can start the last week on time."

He grabbed his coat and flipped off the light as he headed for the exit. Walking down the hall toward the exit to the parking lot, he heard a loud clang come from the manufacturing floor. He made a sharp left and walked through the double doors, entering the manufacturing area.

All the lights were still on but no one was in sight. He scanned the area and heard another clanging noise near the end of Line 5. That's when he spotted her.

"Andrea, is that you?" he called out.

Bolting upright and holding her heart, wide-eyed, Andrea stared in his direction. "Oh jeez, Robbie, you scared me half to death. I thought I was the only one in the building."

"That's what I thought, until I heard you making some noise. What are you still doing here?"

"Oh, God, I just…I don't know. I just want to help the team reach their goals, so I've been staying late for the last few nights trying to clean up these rejects. I've hardly put a dent in them. What are you doing here so late?"

Robbie chuckled. "Pretty much the same thing. The late shipment staging area was overflowing, so I've been packaging up a few every night so we can get caught up before the end of the month."

Now Andrea laughed. "Kinda makes you wish you had a life, right?"

Robbie nodded. "I think I do. It's Friday night, so I thought I'd go out and try to find it."

"Good luck with that," Andrea replied as she gave him a wave.

He turned and went back through the double doors. Two minutes later he reappeared.

"Hey, you gonna be here much longer?"

"I don't know," Andrea said. "I'm getting tired. I'll probably wrap it up in a few minutes. I'll get all the lights, don't worry."

Robbie stared at her. "Why don't you wrap it up *now*? Let me buy you a steak somewhere, and in return you can teach me how to build a bonus program for my employees. I need to light a fire under these guys."

"You mean, like a real meal? No leftovers or TV dinners?"

"Yeah. You game?"

"Heck, I'll come back tomorrow to finish this up. I'm hungry. I'll meet you in the parking lot in three minutes," Andrea said as she headed to her office to get her things.

The server stopped at their table and cleared their plates, dropping off a dessert menu as she did it.

"That was a wonderful meal, thank you, Robbie. I'll get the next one."

Robbie smiled back at her. "It was worth it. I like your idea about tying the guys into a daily goal of zero late shipments. They tend to get tired and start running a little slower during the last hour of the day. I mean, I get it, but having some financial incentive might cure that."

"I thought you were going to say, 'But Bentley won't let me do it.' That's what everybody else says," Andrea said, watching for his response.

"Nah, better to ask forgiveness later than permission now. I like it so I'm gonna do it. Besides, he forbade me to hire replacements for my two stars that left, but he didn't say I couldn't pay my remaining guys more."

Andrea laughed and said, "I like the way you think. My uncle Tyler would like you too."

"Your uncle who?"

"Tyler. He sort of raised me. He used to be an Economics Professor and he coaches me a lot."

"Used to be? What's he do now?"

"He owns a bar on the south side."

Robbie brightened up. "Sounds like my kinda guy. I'd like to meet him someday."

They each took a sip of their wine and tried to drag the evening out. Neither really wanted to leave yet.

"How about a little dessert? I mean, we worked late. We should get a reward, right?" Robbie asked.

Ordering a blackberry cobbler they could share, they took their time finishing dessert and talking about the company. Andrea told him more about the new March bonus program format and why she was changing it. At the end of the night, they both agreed they'd sleep in tomorrow and see each other at work in the afternoon.

For the first time in months, Andrea and Robbie both enjoyed a sound sleep.

WEDNESDAY, FEBRUARY 28

The horn sounded, ending the day and the month for the Manufacturing team. When it sounded, Line 6 was a few minutes away from finishing a shipment. Three team members stayed on past quitting time to make sure it got done and was included in the final count.

Andrea was down on the floor thanking everyone for a good effort during a hard day of work. She shook some hands and patted some backs. As they all started to clear out, she headed for the warehouse to see Robbie. They had worked late every night this week to clean up the rejects and get everything shipped out.

All the workers in shipping had left ten minutes ago, after the last UPS pickup was made. She could see Robbie in his office, but on the floor, she spied what appeared to be the last seven shipments of the day still uncrated, apparently arriving too late to make the final shipment.

Robbie came out of his office and offered his assessment of the situation. "Your folks seemed to be working hard today. Mine were too, but there was just too much. How many did you end up with?"

Andrea frowned a bit and said, "Not enough. Yesterday ended at 2,878. Around ten this morning, I heard a loud cheer from the floor. I ran out there to see what it was, and it was the twenty-second unit of the day, putting us at 2,900. Everyone was cheering making the lower goal."

Robbie smiled. "That was a good sign. Maybe they're getting into it now. I know they cranked out a ton after that because we were all out there trying to crate 'em up and get them shipped out. But they missed the middle target?"

"They kept track after that. Thomas—you know, the guy on Line 6 with the deep booming voice—would call out the number every time they finished one. Two thousand nine hundred and one, two thousand nine hundred and two, and he just kept going all day. Just before the final horn, they hit 3,048. Missed it by two."

"Damn!" Rob said under his breath.

"Well, not your fault. You guys did great, shorthanded and all."

Rob rubbed his chin and looked around. "They counted 3,048, but that includes these seven here that missed the UPS truck. So the report will reflect 3,041, unless…"

Andrea stared at him. "Unless what?"

"How many rejects are out there?"

"I-I don't know. But they aren't counted, so how does it matter?"

"Go check, quick. We may not be dead yet," Rob ordered.

Andrea dashed out of the warehouse and returned five minutes later.

"There's six rejects, Rob," she said between heavy breaths.

"Wanna stay late one more night? I could order a pizza or something."

"What do you have in mind?"

Robbie assumed a sly smile and said, "We've got till ten o'clock to get all these down to the UPS airport site. Pick three of the easiest rejects to repair. Start working on them now. I'll start crating these seven shipments, then I'll crate the three you fix. I drove my pickup truck today. We'll load them into that and run them down to the airport. Then we can count them, and we'll have 3,051."

"Canadian bacon and pineapple for me!" Andrea cried out as she turned and ran back to the reject staging area.

At 8:45 Andrea stared at the third reject she had repaired and was about to box it up and attach the packing slip to it when she saw movement out of her left eye. She swiveled around and saw Stan staring back at her.

"What are you doing here?" he asked.

"I could ask you the same question. How did you get in?"

"I know the night watchman. He unlocked for me. Left my wallet here and I had some brews with the guys nearby and figured I better get it before I drove home."

"You OK to drive?" Andrea asked.

"I'm fine. We ate a lot. What are you doing here?"

"Robbie is in shipping. He's crating the last items up and then we're racing them down to UPS so they can be included in the count."

Stan stared at her. Finally, he mumbled the question, "Why?"

"Why?" Andrea said. "So we could make the middle goal. I've been repairing rejects and this is the last one we need. We have—"

"Andi, hurry up! I'm done with these and just need to crate that last one up. We can write out the UPS waybill on the way down there," Rob yelled.

Bewildered, Stan looked at Robbie at the far end of the building and back to Andrea. "You're staying late so we can get the middle bonus?"

"Stan, everybody worked so hard today, but we were a little short. We're just, you know, giving it a little nudge, that's all."

Stan eyed her a moment, then went to his station and pulled his wallet out of the locker. He gave her a weak little wave and left the way he came in.

Robbie picked up the last reject and said, "Come on, we have to hurry if we're gonna make it."

THURSDAY, MARCH 1

A s the employees rolled in Thursday morning, their eyes were drawn to the white board, which displayed 3,051 in red oversized numbers. Three exclamation points followed.

Andrea waited until nearly everyone was there to turn on the loud speaker and say, "Congratulations to the entire manufacturing team! You made the middle goal and will all see a four-hundred-dollar bonus on your March 5th check. Way to go!"

Robbie and Sammi were standing beside her, enjoying the show. All three of them watched as the employees celebrated. A few—Stan and his friends—and some isolated pockets of employees stood there like stone statues, but the majority were celebrating.

Sammi leaned closer to Andrea and whispered, "When you cut their base pay, that cost them an average of almost $350 each. Now you're replacing it with four hundred bucks. Some of these folks are celebrating breaking even."

"I know. I told them that if they did what they've always done, they'd make the same. And they did. And when they get their check and see that bonus on there, maybe then they'll see we keep our word and start to understand that if they can speed it up, they'll earn more. It's…well, it's a power thing. When they realize *they* have the power to affect the size of their own paycheck, hang on to your hat. Things will explode around here. Today was just one little baby step in that direction."

SATURDAY, MARCH 3

"So I bet you're tired after all that," Tyler said as he poured out two cups of coffee.

"You bet," Andrea said, having no trouble agreeing.

"And now you're changing the March bonus to be based on the number of units produced per day. And you think that will motivate them more?"

"Absolutely. At the beginning of the month, it's not exciting. In fact, it's boring. After one day or one week, they really can't judge whether they are on track or not. So I'm just making the goal smaller and doing it by day. That way there's meaning to every individual job too and they don't lose interest after making one milestone and realizing that there's not enough time to get to the next one. In February we saw that at the end of the month, the next milestone seemed too far away. The employees think they might as well relax and slack off during the last few days, since they won't reach the next goal anyway."

"That should keep them focused," Tyler agreed. "You know, it's funny. In today's world, attention spans are just one more thing that is speeding up."

"Exactly, so now I just have to explain the program well and I think it will be a hit. I mean, it also makes each day a little game. And it sure makes it clear that people who are not working fast or hard are costing everybody else money. I think the peer pressure alone may help kick some of these folks into gear."

Pulling a document out of her briefcase, she said, "Here, take a look at this flyer I made up to explain it."

Tyler read it over. "OK, this is good. It makes it easier to understand. And I like the way you tied it in by doing the math for them and showing them how much they would get. With the payout based on hours worked, you reward good attendance at the same time. You know, you should figure out a way to give them a weekly update. If you can get a work hours report, you could show each employee what they are on pace to make."

"Oh, I like that idea! I could—let me think. I could create an Excel template and all I'd have to do is fill in their name, hours worked by that employee so far this month, the number of units produced and dollar amount in the pool—which would be the same for everybody—and build a formula that computed their share based on total hours worked by the whole team. I could do that!"

Tyler grinned back at her. "I like that too. You could do it over the weekend, and when they showed up for work on Monday morning, every employee could get a personalized report showing the amount they can earn at their current pace."

"Jeez, better stop coming up with ideas for me. I'll have to buy you more chocolate-covered cherries."

Tyler laughed. "I swear, girl. You're getting this whole motivation thing down to an art form!"

MONDAY, MARCH 12

Through Friday, March 9th, the Manufacturing Department had produced 1,196 units and the employees were starting to grasp the daily goal concept much better.

At 8:00 a.m. Monday, as they filed in to work, each employee had an envelope taped to their locker. The first few eyed it a bit fearfully, but after opening it, they were all smiles.

Each envelope contained a half page summary of their bonus status after the first seven days of the work month. It looked like this:

NAME:		SUE ANDERSON		
			WORKING DAYS IN THE MONTH	
MARCH HOURS WORKED		56		
			22	
TOTAL DEPT. HOURS		5,152		
EMPLOYEE PERCENTAGE		1.09%	WORK DAYS SO FAR THIS MONTH	
BONUS DOLLARS IN POOL		$14,448.00	7	

	SUE ANDERSON	
	MARCH BONUS AMT.	MARCH GOAL FOR # OF UNITS PRODUCED
EOM-FORECASTED DOLLARS IN POOL		3,960
AT THE CURRENT PACE	$493.57	
AT 5% IMPROVEMENT PACE	$518.24	UNITS PRODUCED AS OF TODAY
		1,196
AT 10% IMPROVEMENT PACE	$542.92	

As each employee opened it up, their confidence that the bonus program was truly real and on-going increased. Starting out their Monday with details on how much their bonus was likely to be if they kept working at the same pace immediately put everyone into a better frame of mind.

From a distance, Andrea watched to see their reactions and read what she could from them. The three supervisors had all been briefed and were silently observing as well.

At ten o'clock that morning, Reese, Malik, and Meghan came up the stairs to the mezzanine level overlooking the floor and filed into Andrea's office. Andrea signaled Meghan to close the door.

"You all saw the employee summaries today?"

"At first I didn't and I wanted to look, but it was personal to the employee, so I didn't feel right about asking to see it. Then I went into my office and noticed you had made an extra copy for each one of my line workers," Malik said, grinning.

"That's their personnel file copy," Andrea clarified. "File them away after you've taken a look. You need to be in tune with who's getting how much. Those working overtime, by the way, will be making even more as their share of the pot increases."

"That won't take them long to figure out," Reese added. "But I have a question. Are you going to try to make one of those personalized forms for everybody every week?"

Andrea nodded and smiled. "Absolutely. It's great reinforcement for them."

"Doesn't it take a long time to create each one?"

Shaking her head, Andrea replied, "Not at all. In fact, it was way faster than I expected. You see, I just create a template for everyone and save it with all the data pre-filled in. I put in the date, the number of working days for the month and so far, the total department hours, and the bonus dollars in the pool. Then I save it as the master. For each employee, I simply enter their name once and put in how many hours they've worked so far in the month, straight off the daily hours report. Everything else is a formula that Excel fills in. Takes about twenty seconds per employee. I'll show you all how because I'm thinking I'll probably let you each do your own thirty people yourselves."

Reese smiled. "Oh, that's slick. Probably took you longer to put them each in an envelope."

"It did," Andrea admitted. "I'm going to change it so I can fold it and have it display their name through a window envelope so I don't have to write their names on each one."

They exchanged a few ideas about how to organize the process even more, then everyone paused for a moment.

Andrea seized the dead time to ask, "So, any reactions you saw from the crew?"

"All good," Meghan replied. "I mean, usually on Monday everybody's kinda dragging themselves in, thinking about the prospect of another long week. But this morning, whoa! I mean, they seemed kinda fired up. I noticed Malik's Line 1 got cooking right away, and that's always a good start for everybody."

"I think they're starting to believe more, Andrea," Reese said. "This daily bonus calculation is way more engaging than the monthly one. It makes every day much more meaningful."

Malik nodded. "Reese is right. Everybody seems to like it."

Andrea's eyebrows moved up a notch as she stared back at Malik and the others. "Everybody?"

"Almost," Meghan replied quickly. "Stan, Ricky, and his stalwart 'we hate management' buddies club seemed unimpressed. In fact, I saw one of them crumble it up and toss it in the garbage."

Andrea nodded. "That's OK. We can't expect everyone to love the idea. At least not yet. Maybe later."

The supervisors and Andrea continued their discussion for another thirty minutes, then started to break up.

Malik stood up, his long legs seeming to take forever to rise from his seat. "Um, actually, one thing, Andrea."

"Yes?"

"Um, so are we—you know, the supervisors—uh, getting a bonus too?"

Andrea smiled. She'd been waiting for that question. "Here's my plan. If March goes well, and I don't get fired in April for doing this, I think the supervisors should be on a quarterly bonus plan, and I'm working on how we would structure that now."

The room was silent. Meghan finally broke it, asking, "What do you mean, if you don't get fired in April? What's going on?"

Realizing she had said too much, Andrea assumed a calm countenance and focused on putting their minds at ease. "I, um, I have permission from Bentley to do this as a two-month test. At the end of March, it will be reevaluated and there will be a decision then about whether these changes will continue."

Again Meghan verbalized the same question all three of them had. "So, OK, but what does that have to do with you getting fired?"

Andrea looked down at the carpet for a moment, then said, "Well, fact is, I really believe in this, so I'm going to be fighting hard for it. Never know how Bentley will react. I was, um, you know, making a bad joke. Let's keep this two-month-test stuff to ourselves for now, OK?"

Reese started to say something but was interrupted by a loud bellowing from the floor. "Fifty!" Deep-voiced Thomas McCann called out the milestone, and they could hear the cheering below.

THURSDAY, MARCH 15

At 3:15 p.m. on Thursday, the conveyer belt on Line 3 broke down. Dale Weston, the mechanic, was called in, and after three aborted tries, he announced that the line was dead for the day. He was missing a medium size gear, and by the time he traveled to the hardware store and returned with it, it would take too long to fix it and be up and running again before 5:00 p.m.

Reese nearly screamed at him, "I don't get it. Is that an unusual part?"

Dale shook his head and said, "Well, not really, like, unusual. We just used the last one, I guess, and don't have any more in stock. Shit happens. Don't get your panties in a bunch about it."

Reese's eyes grew wide, and for a moment, bystanders were fearful that he would strangle the life out of Dale. Instead, he said, "Go and get the part. Come back as quickly as you can and fix it tonight."

"Might mean some overtime," Dale said.

Reese gave him a look that didn't require interpretation, and the mechanic left quickly.

Looking around, Reese called out, "OK, you know the drill. Everybody move over to Line 4 and we'll piggy back up. Make some room for them and let's try to just keep this going."

Reese noticed a dozen pairs of eyes staring up at the score-board. They were frozen at 158 units, and everyone knew today would not be a record day.

FRIDAY, MARCH 16

Dale knocked tentatively at Andrea's open door and peered in.

"You wanted to see me, ma'am?"

"Come in, Dale. Take a seat," Andrea said.

Andrea wanted to put him at ease, so she started slowly. "You know, Dale, you and I have talked before, but I've never really asked you about your duties or, well, anything. How long have you been with the company now?"

Dale rubbed his chin and looked up at the ceiling. "I guess it's been five years now."

"You seem to know a lot about repair on our equipment. How did you learn that?"

"Well, ma'am, I actually worked on Line 4 for a while, and when one of the lines would break down, I'd pitch in to help. I was pretty good at fixin' 'em quick, so one day Charlie just asked me if I'd like to be the full-time mechanic."

"Oh," Andrea said, quietly, as though that explained a lot.

"So who do you report to?" she asked.

"Well, I used to report to Charlie, but he just kinda left me alone to do my thing. I stayed busy. Sometimes, if nothing was going on, I'd fix his car for him. You know, whatever he wanted. Now, I fix the office machines for the ladies upstairs and take out the trash and stuff."

"So you never really had any training?"

Dale's eyes went wide. "Uh, no, ma'am. Like what?"

"Well, for one thing, you're in charge of the spare parts, right?"

"Uh huh."

"What kind of an inventory system are you using?"

"Um, ma'am, I didn't go to no college. I just kinda picked it up, and I've always been good with my hands—making things and jerry-rigging things. I'm sorry, but, I mean, I don't have no system. I just try to keep us stocked up."

"You still got some good friends on the lines, don't you?"

"Oh, yeah. I know practically everybody," Dale said, smiling.

"That's good, Dale, because from now on you're part of the Manufacturing Department and you work for me. All those folks out there working on the line, they're counting on you to keep things rolling for them. Did you know that we have a bonus program in place for the workers on the line and every time a line goes down, it backs everything up and basically takes money out of their pocket?"

Dale's eyes grew wide and he shook his head. "No! No, I didn't know that."

"So, Reese was thinking that you were a bit unconcerned about the problem yesterday."

"Oh, you mean 'cuz of what I said?"

Andrea looked at him and said, "Yeah, mostly the part about his panties."

"Oh, jeez, I'm sorry. That's just guy talk. I didn't mean nothing by it."

"Well, like you said, you got friends on the lines, and I know now that you know how important it is to all of them. So when you keep the lines up and running, you're helping your pals out."

"I get it. I won't let them down again."

"I know you won't. You're very good at your job, and now you know why it's even more important. So I have one question for you," Andrea said, purposely letting the sentence kind of hang in the air.

"What's that?"

"How'd you like to make a bonus every month?"

SATURDAY, MARCH 17

"Jeez, girl, you've been scarce lately. Whatcha been up to?" Tyler asked as he brought her a plate of fruit and her favorite blueberry treat.

"Where do I begin?" she asked as she enjoyed her first scrumptious bite of the muffin.

Andrea brought her uncle up to date, trying to cover all the events since they last met. She told him about her conversation with the mechanic yesterday and how it wrapped up.

"So he's been operating in a separate department but he wasn't being managed by anyone; he's practically a free agent. No one was monitoring him and, since almost all of his actions directly affect my department, I just told him he's working for me from now on."

"You didn't check with Bentley or Craig first?" Tyler asked.

"Nah," Andrea said, knowing her uncle would be pleased with that response.

Too right, she thought, as Uncle Tyler gave a little fist pump.

"I just signed him up. I don't really have time anymore to ask permission. Besides, I'm not sure the higher-ups even care. And when I offered him a bonus, he was more than amenable."

"A bonus for what? Are you giving him part of the pool that the line workers are sharing?"

"No way," Andrea replied. "I think that would tee them all off. No, I'm giving him a bonus for managing the inventory so we never run out again. I figure if we eliminate breakdowns, that's probably worth a hundred or more units per month."

"How did you structure it?" Tyler asked.

"It's a two-part deal. First of all, I showed him a good way to do inventory so that we never run out of a key part again. I told him when we go a full month without having to order a part to get one of the lines back up, he'll get a two-hundred-dollar bonus."

"It's worth that much to the company?" Tyler asked.

"No. It's worth about ten times that much!"

"So how is he doing the inventory now?"

"Unc, he wasn't really doing it at all. He'd eyeball the supplies and just wing it. So I created a form for him and told him he needed to do inventory of the high volume items twice a month and the low volume items once a month. Here, it's a simple form. Take a look."

She pulled a piece of paper out of her briefcase and handed it over.

JUGGERNAUT INVENTORY

ITEM	# ITEMS ON HAND	# USED PER MONTH	CURRENT DAYS WORTH OF INVENTORY	VENDOR LEAD TIME # OF DAYS TO REPLENISH	MINIMUM EXTRA CUSHION	# NEEDED TO ORDER
ITEM A	4	16	5.00	10	8	14
ITEM B	118	200	11.80	3	100	112
ITEM C	10	4	50.00	7	2	0
ITEM D	38	120	6.33	4	60	76
ITEM E	12	80	3.00	2	40	47

Tyler studied it for a second and said, "OK, I need a quick explanation. Remember, I dealt with generalities at the University—not, you know, real-life details."

"Ooh, I could say so many mean things to that." Andrea' eyes twinkled as she continued, "But I'll pass. Too easy. So, obviously this is a mockup. The item name or description is in the first column. Then he fills in the number of those items currently in stock. The next number is the historical average usage per month of that item. In the column to the right of that, we show the estimated number of days that we have items in stock for. That way, he can scan it and any really low numbers tell him he better hurry up and order."

"OK," Tyler said. "I'm following so far."

"The fourth column is the historical average number of days it takes a vendor to get that part to us. Some are easy and really quick, but some seem to take forever. That replenishment delay number is part of the Excel formula I created to generate the final column."

"Wait," Tyler interrupted. "You skipped one. What is this Minimum Extra Cushion?"

"It's my peace of mind column. I want to know that we are ordering just a little bit more than we likely need. Every item gets a minimum cushion, which is half of our average monthly usage. Then all those numbers factor in, and the last column tells him how many he should order to make sure we never run out in an emergency."

"Just like that? No more parts crisis?" Tyler asked, still staring at the form.

"Well, it requires that Dale does the inventories on time and that he orders correctly. Until he gets the hang of it, I told him I need to approve every order. After a while, he'll figure it out himself and I won't have to micromanage."

"What's the other part of the bonus?" Tyler asked.

"Oh, I want him to be more proactive about making sure everything on the lines is working right—you know, do more preventive maintenance. So I told him I'd pay him three hundred dollars more every month if there were no interruptions of service. If there are, his goal is to make them as brief as possible. I said I would deduct one dollar from that three hundred for every minute a line is down. If he keeps parts in stock, I bet he'll keep the lion's share of that three-hundred-dollar bonus. Every minute saved is a gold mine for us since a minute lost causes the other ninety-two people to totally underperform."

"Sounds like a lot of money to me. He could earn up to five hundred dollars extra every month."

Andrea took another bite of breakfast and agreed, "He could. But, realistically, all the preventive maintenance in the world won't eliminate every little problem. Lines will still go down, but now when he hears about it, he'll come running and do all he can to get it back up quick. Every minute counts so he'll be ultra-focused. And besides that, I've learned that the amount of the bonus needs to be meaningful. In fact, the book I've been reading says that a decent performance—not perfect or fantastic, but decent—needs to reward the worker with a bonus equal to about six to eight percent of their base. If he performs a bit above average, he'll get that. If he does super, he gets more."

Tyler finished his Danish and said, "I like it! Interesting, isn't it?"

"What?"

"The goal you have is to streamline efficiency and make the whole company operate on a faster level. You see how many opportunities there are? Simply by doing a better job of inventory and having an organized maintenance system, you can increase the odds that more units will be produced faster so they get to the customers faster and both your sales and your profits improve."

Andrea cocked her head to the side and said, "Well, yeah. Why is that so interesting? Kind of obvious, isn't it?"

"You don't even recognize what you did," Tyler said, waiting for it to hit her.

"I must be dense this morning. Tell me, Unc, what'd I do?"

"You cannot catch up to the pace of change without restructuring the whole company. In order to become nimble and quick, you have to get every department working together. You just stumbled onto a small department that was under the radar and you moved in and took it over. You absorbed it. Who's next?"

TUESDAY, MARCH 20

Andrea and her uncle continued talking late into the morning on Saturday before he shooed her out the door to prepare for the wild Saint Patty's Day crowd that he was expecting.

Now, three days later, she found herself thinking about how she could influence the other departments to truly get everyone rowing in the same direction. By Sunday afternoon, she had dismissed the thought as inappropriate and far too ambitious for her to take on. But on Monday morning, she awoke with a start and realized it wasn't a crazy idea after all.

Like Unc said, first I have to fight for the hearts and minds of the employees. That battle's still going on, but I'm running out of time. I need to start another hearts and minds campaign, but this time I'm working on the other VPs.

As she headed to work, she was confident she knew exactly where to start.

She had a meeting scheduled at two o'clock with the supervisors, but her notes for that were prepared, so she hiked on over to the warehouse to see Robbie.

She found him helping his crew load up the FedEx truck for their afternoon pickup. She watched as he worked hard, lifting the crates and doing as much, if not more, than his employees.

With the truck loaded, Robbie spied Andrea standing by. He wiped his brow with his forearm and came over to her.

"Hey, how are you? What's up?"

"I owe you a dinner," Andrea said. "I have some ideas and I need a victim I can run them past. Feel like getting some eats tonight—maybe Italian?"

"A victim, huh?"

"You're a good listener. I could ask one of the others if you aren't up to it," Andrea said, smiling mischievously.

"Well, let me think. Sloppy Joes and a beer at home alone watching reruns, or a fine Italian dinner for free with you. Oh, this is a tough one. When and where? I'm going to need to go home and freshen up a bit."

"I'll text you. Somewhere close, say seven o'clock?"

Her dinner plans resolved, she headed back to her office for the 2:00 p.m. meeting. The three supervisors were already seated in her office when she arrived.

"I said two o'clock," Andrea chided good-naturedly.

"It's ten after," Reese said, looking at his phone.

"Oops, sorry," Andrea chuckled. "It's OK, I can make this brief. I've been thinking we need to keep the full-court press on. You know, continue to crank it up. Have you all finished your raise chats with your staff?

"I got one more to go," Meghan said. Malik indicated he was done and Reese said he had two more to do.

Andrea nodded and said, "Anybody seen anyone who has really taken it up a notch since your chat with them?"

"How high up?" Reese asked.

"High enough so that if you gave them a modest bump up in pay, all the other workers on the line would have to admit they understand why. Maybe someone who really improved their game enough in the last two weeks that everyone else, not just you, noticed as well."

"Bingo!" Reese said. "That would describe Manny Chisum on Line 4. I mean, it's not a real big deal, but I told him that he needed to work on his attitude. He's a fine worker—not spectacular, but steady. His problem is he just sort of naturally does a lot of frowning. Not the happiest soul around. He's kinda made everybody else around him quieter and more subdued. That was the *old* Manny. After our talk, I told him that he could act any way he wanted, but he just needed to be aware that people look up to him and he was negatively impacting their workspace. Then I talked about the bonus and how we need to get the whole team working smooth."

Feeling certain she knew where this was going, Andrea prodded him on anyway. "And?"

"He did a one eighty! He is friendlier and smiles more and leaves his frown face at home."

"And you didn't call him in to give him a raise before? He just got the 'this is what you gotta do to get a raise' speech?" Meghan asked.

"Yeah, he got a raise on his anniversary in November, so I told him that he was doing pretty good but he had to work on the attitude thing."

"Well, what are you waiting for?" Andrea asked.

"Jeez, I don't know. I guess I thought it was too soon."

"Reese, it's a great example. I say you should consider calling him in tomorrow and bumping him up," Andrea said, trying to suggest it rather than order it.

"How much, you think?" he asked.

"You tell me," Andrea countered. "Attitude is important, but maybe not as important as improving their work quality and gaining speed. What do *you* think it's worth?"

"Well, it's a hell of a turnaround, and like you said, it's a good way for us to demonstrate we were telling the truth. Maybe thirty cents an hour?"

"I'd be fine with that. Maybe even forty cents," Andrea said.

Reese smiled and said, "I know he'll be pleased. And I know it'll mean something to everyone on the line too."

"Cool! Go for it. Now, Malik, Meghan, keep your eyes open for more opportunities like that. We need to do some more raises, but they still have to be earned." Andrea held their eyes as she said the last part, knowing that giving out undeserved raises led to nothing but trouble.

"Now," Andrea raised her voice as she started in again. "I need you guys to brainstorm and get back to me by the end of the week. I'm going to spend some money on the employees and I need some ideas. Meal events at lunch or after work, performance awards we can give out, team building exercises, maybe a Manufacturing Department jacket we can start doling out on special occasions. Think on it and let's make some decisions by Friday. Ten o'clock meeting. Deal?"

"Bentley's going to let you spend some money for that too?" Malik asked.

"Oh, gee, I don't know. I have a budget for the department that was approved last year. Asking Bentley for permission would be so boring. I think our folks deserve it. Let's just do it."

The three supervisors, all grinning like kids at a theme park, nodded their heads. As they wrapped the meeting up, they could hear Thomas's baritone voice bellowing out from the floor, "That's number one hundred fifty!"

Papa Marino's was packed solid for a Tuesday night, which only made it more obvious that Andrea had chosen wisely.

Robbie and Andrea made small talk for the first twenty minutes before Robbie forced the issue.

"So, I'm ready to be a victim. Tell me what wacky scheme you have in mind now."

Andrea took a sip of her wine, feeling she might need a bit more courage to go forward with the conversation.

Tentatively, she began, "Rob, I feel a bit awkward about this because I'm afraid it will come off as, you know, butting my head into your business. But, the truth is, I know I can only do so much with my department and then a lot of our success or failure ends up depending on you and the other departments. Mostly, though, it depends on logistics, warehousing, and shipping. So I was wondering if you would be willing to listen to a few suggestions I had."

Robbie eyed her, hesitated, then nodded. "Listening never killed anybody."

Andrea let out a sigh of relief. "Thanks. I'm not saying you have to do any of this. I mean, it's all your call, but you've been very kind and helpful so far. Working those late shifts to get all the end-of-February orders out really impressed me and helped immensely. So, even if you hate my ideas, I still owe you big time for helping me out."

Rob nodded. "Go ahead, let's hear your thoughts."

"Well, I was wondering if you might consider putting part of your crew on a later shift, so they could help finish crating up the items and getting them to UPS before the evening deadline. Maybe like—"

"Ten to seven?" Robbie interrupted.

"Yes, I mean, maybe you—"

Robbie put his hand up like a traffic cop signaling stop. "I'm there already. Sort of for a different reason, but it makes a lot of sense. I had a beer with Malik the other night, and I told him about a guy I have, Bernie, who is late every morning but otherwise a solid worker. Malik said he had the same problem. So we got to talking, and I thought I'd switch my guy to a ten-to-seven shift so he could be on time and I'd trade another guy, one Mike for another."

"One Mike for another?" Andrea asked.

"Yeah, Malik's got Mike Albers, who is always late, and I got Mike Langley, who originally applied for a manufacturing line job but there were no openings so we took him in shipping instead. He still wants to work on a line. They're making almost the same amount, so it's almost an even swap. Then I'd put Mike Albers on the ten-to-seven shift with Bernie and they could stay late and finish off the last of the evening's shipments."

"And then they could get those shipments to UPS somehow?" Andrea asked, suppressing the smile she felt ready to erupt on her face.

"Well, actually, I was just thinking that we only really need to do that on the last day of the month in order to make sure the official count of shipments matches your count in manufacturing."

Andrea nodded, then followed with another thought. "That'd be true if all we were worried about was matching up the numbers. But my thought was that if we were able to send them to UPS *every* night before the deadline, then the customers would get them one day sooner and that would help close the gap between us and what the competition is averaging."

"Oh, yeah," Robbie replied. "I forgot. It's not all about us, is it?" He smiled wryly.

"No, but I don't know. Is it even possible? I mean, you can't be transporting the last shipments every night in your pickup."

Robbie's head bobbed, indicating his agreement. "Not only that, but some nights I couldn't even fit it all in. So I was checking out how else I could do it, and there's a courier company in town with vans, called Top Delivery. I got a quote from them for an end of the month run and it wasn't too bad. I bet it'd be even lower if I asked them to do it every night."

Andrea's smile was nearly perpetual now. "That'd be wonderful, and it kinda brings me to my second point. Do you think Gretchen and Sammi would be open to me making some suggestions about what they could do too, to stay in tune with the things we're doing?"

"You got ideas for them too?" Robbie asked.

"Well, our pay-for-performance system may cause some turnover from the, um, less talented personnel, and I have some thoughts on what Sammi could do to bring in a higher quality applicant."

Robbie locked eyes with her and asked, "And you've got something for Gretchen too?"

"Something good! If we can get to the point where we are getting every shipment out the door on the day it's ordered, we could change our advertising and retrain the order-takers and emphasize our speedier service. I think that would put a little charge in sales."

Robbie shook his head as he smiled back at her. "What? The Manufacturing Department isn't keeping you busy enough? Now you have time to work on all the others too?"

Andrea gave a nervous laugh and said, "Probably sounds that way, but we have so little time to turn this ship around. And there's only one thing I know for sure—I can't do it alone. We need to all be in the same boat, rowing in the same direction."

SATURDAY, MARCH 24

obbie made the decision to begin the ten-to-seven shift and do the worker swap on April first. That gave Bernie time to prepare and Mike the chance to participate in the full bonus program for March.

Malik broached the subject with Mike and was pleased to see that his tardiness was bothering him greatly and he had not been able to find an easy solution, so moving to a later shift in another department suited him just fine.

Meanwhile, for the last weeks of March, both Andrea and Robbie continued to stay late and get the last shipments out on the same day they were ordered.

On Saturday, a ritual started coming into shape. Andrea would show up around two in the afternoon and Robbie arrived minutes later. Andrea worked on the reject pile, fine-tuning the remaining shipments, while Robbie finished crating the last jobs from Friday night. When they were done, they picked a new restaurant and went to dinner together.

Seated at their table, Andrea got right to it. "So what else is new in shipping, Robbie?"

"Bernie is psyched up to be able to sleep in starting in April, and Mike Albers came by a couple times on his lunch break to watch what the guys do and get to know everybody. He seems happy too. Well, except for one thing."

"What's that?" Andrea asked.

"He wanted to know if we had a bonus program too."

Andrea eyed her friend cautiously, wondering how he handled the question.

"I told him I was working on it. I said I hope to have one in place by May first."

"Not April?" Andrea pushed.

"Andi, honestly, I don't really understand how to create a program. I figured I'd need more time."

"We all need more time, Robbie."

He nodded. "Yeah, I know, but I honestly don't know where to begin. You got any suggestions?"

"I'll give you one to start with. You base the bonus on one or sometimes two things. Never more than that. And one is best to begin with. So, just think about your priorities and the company's priorities and ask yourself where the employees can make the biggest difference. It has to be something within their control that is one of their primary functions and doing it right or faster or better brings in more revenue or decreases cost. I mean, the whole idea is to bonus them for something that essentially pays for itself."

"Like getting everybody to produce more units in the same amount of time?"

"Yeah, and you know, mine was kinda easy to figure out. Yours may be tougher, but you design it so that it's based on something you can count. Gotta be objective, not subjective."

Robbie mulled that over and replied, "So that way they can influence making the bonus or not and it's not dependent on my whim or subjective feelings, right?"

"Exactly. Anything come to mind?"

"Well, I guess we could do number of items crated every day or month, but they really can't control that. Our goal has always been to crate and ship everything as you send it to us. If you have an off day or sales slack off, then my guys could fail and it wouldn't be their fault."

"That's true," Andrea agreed. "Well, think on it for a few days. You know your business. There's always something."

"Actually," Robbie said, pausing a moment as he thought, "we could base it on the number of items returned due to damage caused by poor packaging. That costs us plenty, and cutting it down would be a seriously good way to reduce expenses."

Smiling back at him, Andrea said, "I like it. Nothing worse to our image than delivering damaged goods."

The two of them finished their dinner and toasted each other with their final drink. An alliance was being forged with every conversation.

MONDAY, MARCH 26

O n Monday, the employees of the Manufacturing Department strode through the main entrance and, with a bit of zip in their step, arrived at their lockers and smiled to see another envelope taped to the front. With vigor, they opened them quickly and responded. A few let out a low whistle; many more just glanced at the person nearest them and smiled.

The mounted whiteboard out on the floor showed the unit count at 3,084 and the new monthly pool total at $40,807.00. Every full-time employee working exactly eight hours a day saw the same numbers as Sue:

JUGGERNAUT ENTERPRISES - MANUFACTURING DEPT. EMPLOYEE BONUS STATUS
as of March 23rd

NAME:	SUE ANDERSON		
			WORKING DAYS
MARCH HOURS WORKED	136		IN THE MONTH
			22
TOTAL DEPT. HOURS	12,508		
EMPLOYEE PERCENTAGE	1.09%		WORK DAYS SO FAR
			THIS MONTH
BONUS DOLLARS IN POOL	$40,807.00		17

	SUE ANDERSON		
			MARCH GOAL FOR
	MARCH BONUS AMT.		# OF UNITS PRODUCED
EOM-FORECASTED DOLLARS IN POOL			3,960
AT THE CURRENT PACE	$574.20		
			UNITS PRODUCED
AT 5% IMPROVEMENT PACE	$602.90		AS OF TODAY
			3,084
AT 10% IMPROVEMENT PACE	$631.61		

With smiles all around, Andrea walked halfway down the stairs from the mezzanine level and made a brief announcement before the motors on the lines were turned on.

"You should all be seeing the results of the bonus program so far. We are well ahead of last month's pace, and I am so impressed with each and every one of you.

"The supervisors and I want to reward you in every way we can, so I wanted to tell you all that we've decided to purchase some awesome Juggernaut Enterprises leather jackets for each one of you, which will be given out for specific performance events as a personal reward. Reese, Malik, and Meghan will have more details later about how that will happen.

"I also want to tell you that we've decided to make a series of videos showing the best way to perform each function. Every one of you has a different style and a different take on creating a work of art as it moves along the assembly line. We're going to identify those individuals who everyone agrees is doing a superb job and create a training video featuring that person. It may take some extra hours to do it, but everyone featured will be paid. And then, when new employees join our lines, we'll use the videos to train them step by step. It should be fun, and it should help us determine best practices so we can move the lines faster and pay everyone more bonus money.

"OK, turn those engines on and let's get cranking! We've still got five more days in March to shoot for the records. Only 876 units to go to reach our goal of 3,960, and only 916 to go to do something that hasn't been done in four years—get to four thousand! Let's roll!"

The engines turned on, and 118 minutes later, Andrea could hear Thomas intoning, "That's fifty!"

FRIDAY, MARCH 30

A t 2:40 in the afternoon, Thomas called out, "One hundred and sixty!" The team had reached 3,951 for the month. A huge cheer rose up, as they knew they would surely make their goal and a nice fat bonus along with it.

Six minutes later, the lights in the building went dark. The backup generator came on, lighting the emergency exits and the hallways.

"What's happening?" several people yelled out at the same time.

Reese hustled out to the main office and stepped outside. Traffic lights were out all over the neighborhood. Employees from other companies wandered out of their offices, a look of bewilderment on their faces as well.

Reese pulled his cell phone out and called the power company. A rapidly placed recording said that several areas of the city were experiencing a blackout that started at two o'clock and was spreading to more neighborhoods. There was no estimate yet of when the power would be restored.

Andrea came down the stairs carefully, watching her feet at every step. Reese came back and reported the news to everyone.

Andrea took a few steps back up and in her loudest voice called out, "Everyone, stay calm. It's just a blackout. City Light is working on it and it could go back on any minute. Or not. We don't know yet. Find a seat or get some fresh air and we'll get back to work as soon as the power is restored."

At four o'clock, a message went out from the power company stating that their area would not gain power back before nine o'clock tonight.

"What does that mean, Andrea?" Stan asked, snarling. "Do we get paid until five?"

Before she could answer, Stan's buddy, Ricky Stamper, yelled out, "And what about the bonus? We didn't get to the goal. Are you going to screw us out of our bonus now too?"

"Stan, Ricky, and everybody. I'll handwrite in five p.m. for all of your finish times, and I'm sure power will be restored by tomorrow. I'll make sure you make the goals and get a full bonus. This is kind of a downer, but everyone did great this month and a few minutes in the dark can't change that. Enjoy your weekend. See you on Monday—in April!"

She watched as they all filed out to end the day. Robbie appeared out of the darkness to stand beside Andrea. She glanced at him and grimaced.

"This kinda sucks, doesn't it? I was looking forward to a mini celebration at five o'clock."

"Me too," Robbie said. "And I'm afraid I have more bad news for you."

"What now?"

"With the power out, the bay doors are stuck in the down position. When UPS shows up at five, we can't load him up. All of today's shipments are still sitting on the dock. We won't be able to get any of them out, so they don't count."

Andrea pressed her eyes closed and stood silently for a moment. Quietly, she said, "Saturday is still a day in March. If we get these orders left over from today, we can still make our goal. I'll be in here tomorrow sometime after nine." She looked at him, hoping she'd hear what she needed to hear.

Robbie nodded and said, "See you then."

As he walked away, she realized he was the only one in this company she could count on.

SATURDAY, MARCH 31

Saturday morning at 8:45, Andrea passed by the security guard at the entrance and waved. He was getting used to seeing her on the weekends and it didn't shock him that she showed up again this Saturday.

Andrea had called her uncle and rescheduled their Saturday breakfast for Sunday at one o'clock, a few hours before the bar opened. When she told him why she was canceling the Saturday meeting, he seemed unsurprised as well.

Arriving on the floor of the manufacturing area, she was disappointed to see only two items in the reject pile.

"I should be happy," she mumbled to herself. "I'm always harping on them to focus on quality so we can cut down the rejects, and now they did."

Nothing to gripe about here, Andi. Except I'll be here all day now. We need nine more units produced to make the monthly goal and it looks like I'll have to walk seven of them up and down six lines. Ugh.

She checked her watch and again talked out loud to herself, "Robbie should be here in an hour or so. Get to work, girl."

Just before ten o'clock, Robbie entered the room and called out to her, "Hey, looks like you're on the last reject now. Done already?"

"I wish. There were only two of them. We need seven more units done. I'm going to be here another six, seven hours trying to run these all through the lines. Better start collecting the orders and bringing the pieces out here."

"Jeez, Andrea, we've gotta get these loaded up in the Top Delivery van by four or they won't make the Saturday UPS cutoff. We haven't got till ten like on weekdays."

Andrea shook her head and said, "I don't know how I can do it that fast." Her voice whining a bit, she continued, "It just can't—" She stopped talking as she heard more footsteps coming down the hall.

Malik and Meghan walked in. "See, I told you they'd be here," Meghan said, her voice carrying throughout the building. Smiling broadly, she said, "What? Do you think you two can do everything by yourselves? We're thinkin' you need some experienced hands to run these lines."

Andrea grinned back at her. "I was just trying to figure out how I was—" She stopped talking again as Reese walked in, followed by Carol, Thomas, Sue, Paula, and three others she didn't recognize by name.

Reese called out, "Looks like we're still nine units short. Let's get these lines running!"

Andrea looked at all the workers and said, "Guys, I really appreciate you being here, but I can't authorize any overtime."

"We're doing this for kicks, Andrea. We love it here and we don't wanna miss our goal. Besides, Robbie promised us that he'd take us all out for pizza as soon as we were done."

"He did, did he?" Andrea said, staring at Robbie and chuckling. "Always thinking about food. That's Robbie. Well, hell, let's get to work then!"

An hour later, Mike Albers showed up and told his new boss, Robbie, that he needed some more practice crating. Together, the team produced the nine units needed and five more just for good measure. As they finished the last one, Thomas bellowed out, "Three thousand nine hundred and sixty-five!" Everyone clapped.

Top Delivery sent a sixteen-foot box truck to pick up all of Friday's UPS jobs along with the extras created today and was headed to the airport by quarter to four. Having reached their March goal, there were smiles all around.

Andrea looked to Robbie and said, "Hope you brought a truck load of money. These people worked hard and deserve a lot of pizza."

As they left the building, laughing and joking, Andrea imagined a crew shell on the river, and for just a brief moment, she thought she saw them all willingly rowing in the same direction.

SUNDAY, APRIL 1

"**B**acon and eggs again?" Andrea asked.

"Yeah, my cholesterol count was too perfect, so I thought I'd bring it back up," Tyler said, smiling.

"Your doctor would be so proud of you," Andrea deadpanned.

"Enough about my health. Eat your fruit salad and tell me about the exciting stuff happening at Juggernaut."

Andrea brought him back up to speed and ended her summary with yesterday's events and the surprise help she got from the supervisors and workers.

Handing Tyler a copy of one of the end-of-month March bonus summaries, she said, "Take a look at how much an average full-time employee got."

JUGGERNAUT ENTERPRISES - MANUFACTURING DEPT. EMPLOYEE BONUS STATUS
as of March 31st

NAME:	SUE ANDERSON			
			WORKING DAYS	
MARCH HOURS WORKED	176		IN THE MONTH	
			22	
TOTAL DEPT. HOURS	16,223			
EMPLOYEE PERCENTAGE	1.08%		WORK DAYS SO FAR	
			THIS MONTH	
BONUS DOLLARS IN POOL	$45,872.00		22	

	SUE ANDERSON			
			MARCH GOAL FOR	
	MARCH BONUS AMT.		# OF UNITS PRODUCED	
			3,960	
YOUR MARCH BONUS AMOUNT	$497.66			
			UNITS PRODUCED	
			AS OF TODAY	
			3,965	

Her uncle looked it over and let out low whistle. "Wow! Typical worker got almost five hundred dollars. That's big enough to keep them focused, isn't it?"

"You bet! And the best part is, it makes financial sense. We produced an extra 187 units over the average, at twenty-two-percent labor cost. That's well lower than our normal goal, so we not only did it faster, but we also did it cheaper. Yet everybody won—the employees, the company, *and* the customers."

Tyler thought on that and very seriously said, "You've done well, Andi. And it's an outstanding sign when you get hourly employees helping out for nothing more than a camaraderie-packed pizza party. You've accomplished a lot in two months."

"I think so too," Andrea agreed. "Well, that sounded sort of vain, but I'm really pleased with the results. Now I have to go in and see Bentley and find out if he feels the same way."

"What's your read on him?"

"I have no idea. Part of me thinks he'll complain about the extra cost and then let me keep doing my thing. But another part of me calls that wishful thinking."

Tyler concurred. "Do your math. Make sure you are armed with how much extra you paid out and how much more you produced. Look at the previous six months of labor cost, units shipped, and revenue earned and do the math. Compare the cost per unit and the revenue per hour worked to what you did during those two months. I'll bet you come out on top."

"I've got access to all the reports and I can do that tonight from home. I'll print it up so he can see for himself."

Her uncle nodded. "You've still got lots to do."

Andrea eyed him. "What would you recommend?"

"To save the company?" It was a question, but he wasn't asking for an answer. "To save it, you have to get all the departments working in concert with you. This is the fun part. Once Bentley agrees that you did fine and can continue on, you just vaulted yourself into a leadership position. While everyone else was sitting on their hands—"

"Robbie wasn't," she blurted out, interrupting him. "He cut costs, changed shift schedules to match our output, and worked his brains out the last two months."

Giving her an odd look, Tyler continued, "OK, while *almost* everyone else was sitting on their hands, you made dramatic changes and tackled the biggest problem the company had—how to increase productivity. You'll have momentum on your side and you should take advantage of it and get Marketing and HR, in particular, to dovetail their operations with yours."

Andrea finished her coffee, deep in thought. "It seems, I don't know, a bit presumptuous."

Tyler nodded. "Fortune favors the bold."

Smiling back, Andrea asked, "Who said that?"

"Virgil, the Roman poet."

"Hmmm," Andrea said, mulling it over. Quietly, in a voice an octave above a whisper, she added, "Sounds more like famous last words to me."

MONDAY, APRIL 2

The morning of the second was chilly at 7:25 as Andrea parked in the lot and walked into the Juggernaut Building. She organized her schedule for the day and pondered when she would request a meeting with Bentley to discuss her first two month's numbers.

The employees filed in just before eight and, as was her new custom, she perched herself on the mezzanine level and observed them as they opened their envelopes taped to their locker doors. From her angle she could only see about half of the employees, but the reactions were all positive.

She was imagining the meeting she planned to have with everyone later today, offering them the chance to pick their own goals. She had created three versions to pick from: a modest goal version with modest bonuses; a more challenging version, much like the March goals; and an aggressive sort that set higher goals with appropriately high bonus amounts. She was looking forward to seeing which one they would select.

As she made another note on her weekly to-do list, her intercom sounded its tone and Mr. Bentley's secretary said, "Ms. Lane, Mr. Bentley requests your presence in five minutes."

Holding down the lever, she responded, "Thanks, JoAnn, I'll be there."

Suddenly, an unpleasant feeling rose from the pit of her stomach and she felt a sense of trepidation. *He didn't waste any time.*

That makes me think he's either delighted and can't wait to tell me or he's looking forward to firing my ass. Somehow the first option doesn't seem likely. Since when have I ever seen him delighted?

Andrea gathered up her file with the complete data comparison and headed down the hall to the Chairman's office.

She entered and was told to wait in the outer office with Sarah for a moment. That moment stretched into twenty minutes as Andrea caught JoAnn stealing glances at her from time to time. *Like she's looking at a corpse,* Andrea thought.

At the twenty-third minute, JoAnn's intercom buzzed and Bentley bellowed, "Send her in."

Andrea shook off the doubt she felt, pasted a smile onto her face, and entered the room.

"Sir, you requested to see me."

"I know what I did," he snapped back.

Andrea moved to the only chair facing his desk and started to sit down.

"You can remain standing. This won't take long," Bentley said.

Andrea froze where she was and prepared herself for the worst.

Bentley stared at her and said, "I gave you two months and you managed to cost me $82,672 in extra bonuses and I'm calling a halt to this nonsense. The terms of our deal stated that if I was unhappy with your results, you would resign, and, well, I'm very unhappy."

"Sir, I've worked the numbers and—"

Breaking in brutally, Bentley said, "I didn't ask you to speak. I brought you here to tell you that I'm not unhappy." Bentley paused for a moment, then continued, "I'm mortified. I'm stunned that one of my own VPs could do so much damage in such a short period of time. I will want your resignation on my desk before noon. Is that clear?"

Andrea stared back at him. "May I speak?"

Bentley gave a backhand wave as if to say, "Whatever."

"Sir, while the bonuses were indeed a total of $82,672, that was not all *extra* cost. You may remember that when I started the bonus program, I cut everyone's base pay by ten percent. With the average Manufacturing Department worker making $3,400 per month, and with ninety-two workers, we actually cut costs by $62,560 during the two months."

"That doesn't count. We never had bonus programs before, so that 82K in bonuses is all new expense."

"Sir, we'll want to be accurate when we calculate this, so if we are not in agreement, I'll have to ask for a third opinion from a CPA. The agreement we have said I must resign if you are unhappy with results, but you have to have correct numbers to work with and my numbers are very different than yours. Sir, in two months, my crew completed 7,016 units. That was in forty working days. The previous forty working days produced 6,829 units. We made 187 more. Our average revenue per unit last year was $395. Times 187, we generated $73,865 in extra revenue. That more than paid for the extra twenty thousand or so of costs."

She handed him a document showing all of her math.

Bentley stared at it for a second and said, "Smoke and mirrors. I doubt this math is right. Besides, you started out this new policy of giving out raises to anyone at any time. Nonsense, absolute nonsense. And did you count the supervisors in this analysis?"

"No, I didn't. They are on the management payroll and I—"

"No, that would have been inconvenient for you, wouldn't it, Ms. Lane? You cost me plenty when you fired Charlie."

"Actually, sir, Reese replaced him and is making six thousand a month less. I should include those numbers in my computations. A CPA would."

"All right, we will include them. And we'll include the severance I gave him which was for three more months too. See how you like that."

Feeling defeated but not ready to give up yet, Andrea said, "Sir, I know that change is a scary thing for, well, everyone, but we have made remarkable strides in a short period of time. The goal was to increase production, sales, and profits between now and July. The employees are becoming much more involved now and they care more and they're working their hearts out. Getting more production every day at basically the same or lower cost per unit is a great achievement. I ask you, please, to give me a few more months so that the results will be evident to you and others."

Bentley blustered back, "Are you saying I'm too dense to understand the numbers?"

"No! No, sir," Andrea quickly backpedaled. "I'm just saying two months isn't a very long period of time. If we went another month or two, then the data would show up more completely on the Juggernaut Quarterly Report. Please, sir, we're on the right track."

Bentley pursed his lips and sat down in his chair. After a few moments, he muttered, "I'll have Tim look at this and give me his opinion too. Then I'll inform you of my final decision by the end of the day."

Feeling like she had already used every arrow in her quiver, she reached back and found one more she could fling at him. "Sir, we have twenty-one work days in April. Normally, we might produce 3,600 units in that time. You let me stay and I'll produce four thousand for you. At a lower cost per unit than you've ever done before."

"Four thousand?"

"Yes, sir."

He rubbed his chin and said, "I'll let you know."

Andrea had been in her office with the door closed for two hours. Finally, a soft knock on the door caught her attention. Opening it just a crack, Meghan poked her head in and asked, "Got a minute?"

Andrea just nodded. Then, trying to perk up for appearance's sake, she smiled and asked, "What's up?"

"Andrea, everybody on the floor is asking what the new goal is for April. I mean, *everybody*."

Rubbing her forehead, she realized she probably would have to rethink her original goal setting plan. "I'm working on it. I should have something by tomorrow. I'm sorry, other things came up."

"You OK?" Meghan asked.

"I'm good. I'll have info tomorrow for you."

Not certain she got the answer she hoped for, Meghan nodded and left. She closed the door behind her.

Called back into Bentley's office at 4:15, Andrea showed up with nothing more she could use as a counter argument. She knew she was virtually at the Chairman's mercy now.

She entered his office, and this time, he motioned for her to take the chair.

He locked eyes with her, held that for a moment, and said, "I had Tim look over the numbers. And I had him calculate the extra costs per unit and we came to the conclusion that your system cost the company $67,000."

Andrea nearly choked trying to respond.

"Now, Tim pointed out how that included the extra pay for three months of severance for Charlie, and I've generously decided that since that was my decision, I won't make you pay for that. That shaves off $36,000, counting his benefits and all. So, to be more accurate, now you've cost the company $31,000."

Andrea swallowed hard and replied, "Mr. Bentley, I ask one more time that you reconsider. Don't you see the positive direction we are going in? I think it deserves another chance."

"Are you trying to tell me you don't think that $31,000 is a serious amount of money?"

"Sir, I'm sure Tim is doing a good job, but I honestly don't see how that is possible. We normally run a forty-two-percent profit on cost of goods. The extra 187 units generated far more than the extra twenty thousand or so in labor cost. I really think—"

"Enough!" Bentley roared. "Tim said you'd say something like that. What is it with you? You want this job so bad that you're begging now?"

Andrea pressed her eyes closed. *He's right. I am begging. I must be—*

Before she could finish her thought, Bentley said, "So, I'm a fair man. More than fair. You said you could do four thousand units in April. I say hogwash. We haven't done four thousand in over three years and we had more people then. But I tell you what I'm gonna do. I'll give you one more month, if you're willing to work for another fifty percent cut in pay. If you make four thousand units in April and they come in under the normal manufacturing labor cost of twenty-eight percent, then I'll consider letting you stay on here at that same level of pay until July when the bank decides. If I'm not happy or you miss either of those goals, then I'll want your immediate resignation."

Andrea stared back at him, her mind racing a mile a minute. *This is crazy. I should cut my losses now and get out of here while I can. Can he do this? Is it even legal? I should just walk out. I should just—*

Interrupting her own thoughts, she abruptly stood up and, without thinking, from somewhere deep inside her, replied, "You want four thousand, you'll get four thousand. I'm in. I'm all in."

TUESDAY, APRIL 3

On the morning of the third, Andrea got off to a fast start, arriving at her office at 6:30 a.m. She made some notes, checked her to-do list to see what she had scheduled for today and then added several more projects.

At 8:15, she called her three supervisors into her office and wasted no time getting right to it.

"So, I didn't get fired and we've got ourselves another month to convince upper management we're on the right track," she said, smiling broadly.

The eyes of all three supervisors widened.

Meghan spoke up and said, "Um…you mean, you're serious? You really thought you might get fired?"

Realizing she had verbalized her own feelings without thinking, Andrea started to backtrack. "Oh, no, I meant…" Her voice trailed off. She leaned back in her chair, pushed her head back for a second so she was staring at the ceiling, and then resumed her position, looking back at her team.

"You know, you three are grown-ups, so I'm going to treat you like it. I'm going to tell you the truth and you will keep it to yourselves, OK?"

The three nodded.

"The company is in worse trouble than I presented to the workers back in February. I'm not going to go into more detail than that because I'm not even supposed to be telling you this much, but suffice it to say that we have to improve operations significantly and very fast. Anything less than that and things will get worse. Do you want me to go on, or would you rather go on working in uninformed bliss?"

She knew the answer to that question before she asked it, and they all agreed they wanted to hear more. She told them about her ideas of how to improve production and how they were dismissed multiple times before. She explained her original two-month agreement, her pay cuts, and how being fired was, truly, a distinct possibility.

All three supervisors listened in equal parts horror and disbelief.

"So that brings us up to today. See, I sorta made a promise in order to entice Bentley to give me one more month. I promised we'd produce four thousand units this month. If we don't, and if we don't keep labor cost under the usual twenty-eight percent, then I have to resign immediately."

She stopped talking and waited for their response. No one said anything.

Finally Reese spoke up. "So you bet your career that these changes would work?"

"Seemed like a good idea at the time," Andrea said, trying hard to make light of it. It missed the mark.

"Four thousand in twenty-one days is a lot," Meghan said.

"And we already lost a day and a half before we've even announced the goal," Malik added.

"I believe in these guys. They work their tails off and they're focused on the goals. I think we just need to bring it up another notch and make it worth their while if they do it."

"What do you have in mind?" Reese asked.

Andrea smiled and said, "I'm gonna channel my inner Don Corleone and make them an offer they can't refuse. When we break for lunch at noon, tell everyone I need them to stay until 12:15 so I can fill them in on the goal. Then they can break until 12:45."

Their game plan agreed to, the supervisors were reminded once again to keep the seriousness of the problem to themselves. They headed down to the floor.

At 12:01, Andrea walked down the steps from the mezzanine, carrying a large bag, and stopped five steps from the bottom so they could all see her. She passed a wad of flyers down to Meghan and told her to distribute them when she gave the signal.

When the noise level subsided, Andrea spoke as loudly as she dared so that all could hear. "First of all, congratulations on a terrific March. Everyone in the company is talking about it. The 3,965 units was an amazing performance. Now we've raised the bar a bit, but, frankly, there are people in this company who don't believe in you like I do. I think we have a great team here and we can keep winning.

"Dale is on board and he has a new inventory system and some extra motivation." She smiled and rubbed her thumb and fingers together, symbolizing cash, and continued, "So the lines won't break down again for any extended period of time. In fact, with the extra preventive maintenance he is doing, it seems likely they won't break down at all.

"Your supervisors are making every effort to get everybody on the lines in the right spots so you can excel, and they are always doling out raises as you show you deserve them, so we've made changes to reward top performance better and more frequently, and now I believe we're ready to roll."

Andrea nodded to Meghan, and the supervisors began passing out the April bonus details.

The April Bonus Program

Our goal for the month is 4,050 units. The dollars added to the bonus pool are based on the number of units you finish by end of business each day—that is, quality-inspection-passing units. To make that goal, we need to average 193 units or more per day. Here is the way the daily bonus amount will be calculated:

Units shipped	$ added to the bonus pool for each unit
1-50	$10.00
51-100	$11.00
101-140	$12.00
141-160	$13.00
161-180	$14.00
Over 180	$22.00

Completing 4,050 would build the pool up to about $49,950. Every extra order after 180 per day adds $22.00 to the pool. If you work the average number of hours, your share of the bonus pool would be around $540.

Additionally, every day we top 200 units, I will give a brand new Juggernaut Leather jacket out to ten of the workers, names drawn randomly. And just to sweeten this deal, more, if we top 4,100, I will give each of you a crisp $100 bill on the day we do it—my personal thank you for an incredible performance.

"Our goal this month is 4,050 units completed by April 30th. Very few people other than us believe that is even possible. I've tweaked the formula so the reward for making that goal is even higher and will put more money in your pockets than ever before. Any questions?"

The workers were still busy reading the document, but a few cheers and squeals could be heard. One of the employees in the back yelled out, "I want me one of those jackets. Can we see 'em?"

Anticipating that, Andrea had one folded in the bag next to her. It was the one she earned years ago when the company gave out many as rewards. The hundred she had ordered ten days ago were still a few days away. She pulled it out and showed it around.

"We've got one for everybody, all sizes. All we have to do is break two hundred ten times to make sure each one of you gets one. So, now, you go eat your lunch and relax and then let's turn on the jets and make some manufacturing magic happen!"

Some whoops and cheers could be heard. Andrea stole a glance at Stan, leaning on the assembly line along with Ricky. She caught him looking at her and smiling a strange smile. He shook his head and appeared to chuckle as he walked away to the break room.

SATURDAY, APRIL 7

Her breakfast meeting with Uncle Tyler started promptly at ten and ended earlier than usual. The spring weather had been so pleasant that she chose to walk the mile from home to the Professor's Bar. Now, as she strolled back, she replayed some of their conversation in her head.

"You accepted those terms? Just like that?" Tyler asked.

"It sorta just popped out of my mouth. Fact is, I really believe in these people. Once you start tying their goals and ambitions into the goals of the company, it's not such a fight to get people on board. I bumped up the goals and I believe they'll bring it up a notch and reach them."

Tyler shook his head. "It's a hell of a gamble, Andi. I love it! But do you think maybe this is just a short-term period of high intensity? Maybe they'll feel like they can't maintain this pace in the long run?"

"I know. I thought about that, but the reality is there *is* no long run unless we do something radically different. I bumped up the rewards to psych them up this month because if we don't make four thousand, I'm sure to be fired and they'll have to go back to the old pay method. This has to work in order for us to move forward with a pay-for-performance model. And I think that is the only way to consistently ratchet up productivity—which is what will keep us in business. Oh, and more important than that, we've changed the raise procedure, which encourages everyone to bring their A game to work every day; we've moved personnel to more productive spots; and we've decreased the odds that a line will go down and cost us productivity. If we were just trying to make this happen, month after month, by psyching people up, then that would be a flawed strategy."

Tyler nodded as he stuffed some more scrambled eggs in his mouth. "Ever notice how I cleverly ask you difficult, open-ended questions like that?"

Smiling knowingly, Andrea said, "Yeah."

"Why do you think I do that?"

"So you can eat more while I talk."

Tyler laughed. "Exactly! See how well it works."

Andrea laughed with him.

"Actually," Tyler continued, "I like to hear you reason it out, you know, out loud. Sometimes we *think* things and they seem reasonable, but when you *say* them out loud to someone else, that's when you really put the logic to the test. A good solid plan will stand on its own. A bullshit plan will start to fall apart."

Andrea sipped her tea and enjoyed the feeling of confidence that her uncle always gave her.

"There's something else I think that is going on, too, Andi," Tyler said.

"What's that?"

"Because of the deadline the bank gave you, you adopted the management imperative that all the focus has to be on increasing productivity. So now you've put plans into action, all focused on *that*. Delinking raises and reviews, creating a monthly bonus program, tackling the maintenance issues, getting rid of the deadwood like Charlie, and treating the employees better—all those things are happening because you're focused. At some other time in the future, you may need to focus on sales or quality control, and you can use some of these same full-court-press tactics to attack those issues as well."

"I get it. But I'm not in charge of sales, so Gretchen will have to do that."

"I know. And isn't she the one you said was a good salesperson but not a very original thinker? What happens if her department falls down on the job? If you don't have orders to produce, all the productivity in the world won't help you. Remember, nothing happens until someone sells something."

As she turned onto 27th and headed the last few blocks to her home, it was that last part of the conversation that troubled Andrea the most. *He's right. If Gretchen falters and we don't get the sales rolling in, we're all screwed.*

MONDAY, APRIL 9

Gretchen and Andrea took their seats at a corner table at Marie's Diner on 12th Street. They placed their orders and settled in.

"This is nice, Andrea, thanks. I usually take a few minutes and grab a bite at my desk and, of course, the phone rings and people come in and, well, you know."

Andrea nodded. "Too well. I thought it'd be nice to get away and talk one-on-one without interruptions. Plus, I think I have some good news for you."

"Oh, please, I'm ready for some good news," Gretchen replied.

"Well, it's pretty simple," Andrea began. "Working more closely with Robbie, in the warehouse, he sees the marketing advantage of getting every shipment out on the same day it's ordered. So he's moved hours around and added a late pickup at seven o'clock, giving us enough time to crate up the last shipments of the night and bust them on down to UPS."

Andrea stopped there and waited expectantly. She kept waiting, but Gretchen kept staring back at her.

"Gretch, as I understand it, right now we take the orders and give them an approximate date for delivery, right?"

"Yeah," Gretchen said.

"Well, now, with us getting every shipment out on the same day it's ordered before four o'clock, your operators can commit to a delivery date that is spot on unless the carrier drops the ball. Plus that delivery date will probably be one or two days earlier than the estimate. This helps us close the gap a bit between us and our competitors."

Gretchen reached up and touched her throat. "Oh! Oh, of course. Yes, that would be so much better. We get comments every day from buyers asking why it takes so long. That'd be great!"

"Robbie's department is doing most of the work here, but the workers on the line are much more motivated now to get the units completed and they've been doing a great job, so I'm confident we can do it."

Their lunch arrived, and they spent a few minutes on small talk until Andrea felt the time was right.

"Gretch, how are your salespeople doing? Sammi told me you were almost at wit's end with a few of them."

Gretchen shook her head. "It's like they never learn. I show them how to close a deal and they nod and say they'll use that method, and then they blow it the next time too. The retailers need some good hand holding to place an order, and two reps in particular never seem to get it."

"Do you think the commission is high enough?" Andrea asked, trying to steer the conversation toward incentives.

"They're all on salary. We tried the commission thing, but everybody wanted the big accounts and there was a lot of infighting and, well, it was tiring. I just changed them all to salaried and now we don't have to waste any time on that."

Fighting off the urge to choke on her food, Andrea asked, "If you could create a bonus plan or commission structure that was fair and truly motivated them to do well, do you think they'd perform better?"

"I tried. It didn't work. I don't know what else to do," Gretchen admitted as she plowed back into her salad.

They ate and talked for another thirty minutes about the sales reps' issues, then discussed the company website and online marketing efforts. By the time they concluded their lunch, Gretchen had given Andrea the green light to make any suggestion she had concerning the sales reps' incentives and updating the online marketing.

With her head already spinning with ideas, they walked back together to the Juggernaut Building.

Buoyed by her modest success getting Gretchen to open up, Andrea stopped by Sammi's office and suggested they go out and have a drink after work. She spent an hour and half discussing HR, hiring challenges in today's world, and training issues, walking away with another green light to make some suggestions down the road. She spent the evening at home doing online research and jotting down every random thought that popped up regarding sales or human resources.

SATURDAY, APRIL 14

Feeling bad about sponging off her uncle's generous spirit every weekend, Andrea took him out for breakfast at a competitor's bar two blocks away.

"Gotta tell ya, I don't like the idea of spending our money to help a competitor," Tyler said, only half-kidding.

"Now, now, Unc. Maybe you can learn something here."

"I'm too old to learn," he snapped, laughing as he said it.

"Your competitor is serving breakfast and this place is pretty packed. Give you any ideas?"

"Yeah, it gives me the idea I may have to work harder and put in more hours. I'm not sure I want to learn how to do that. So, since I can't do any learning here, how about you tell me all about your adventures this week?"

Andrea filled him in on the meetings with Gretchen and Sammi and told him about the positive reaction that the jacket giveaway had gotten.

"On the tenth, we had our first day breaking two hundred! At the end of the day, I drew ten names randomly out of a hat and we gave a jacket to each of those people. Eventually everyone will get one as long as we break two hundred a total of ten times, but it was still exciting and the winners really showed off. They're pretty nice jackets, and it came out of our budget for promotions that was already OK'd. Since then, we've broken two hundred on the 12th and 13th too, and morale is sky high."

"It's great for team spirit, Andi. A good move!"

"Thanks. It's been fun for everybody. Oh, and Stan won on Friday and I personally went over and put his on him. Just the right size too."

"Is he coming around?" Tyler asked.

"I don't know, but he doesn't seem all mad now. That's something, I guess."

They got a refill of coffee and took a few more forkfuls of their meals. Tyler, talking through a mouthful, asked, "So what ideas did you have for HR and Sales?"

"Take a look," Andrea said, shoving two documents over to him that showed her bullet-point lists of ideas she wanted to share with them.

He did a double take at the length of both lists. Coughing, he managed to say, "I guess your creative juices must have been flowing. This is a lot."

Andrea smiled at the compliment and added, "I'm going to sit down with each of them and explain all of the ideas I have and see which ones take root."

"Can I make a suggestion?" Tyler asked.

"Fire away."

Tyler leaned toward her and, in a conspiratorial voice, he whispered, "Don't do it! Do *not* show them this list."

Andrea stiffened and said, "Why not?"

Tyler shook his head. "Andrea, did you miss school on the day they taught you about business etiquette?"

Andrea cocked her head and gave him a funny look. "Too much?"

"Yup. What you're really saying here is, 'Gretchen, Sammi, everything you're doing is wrong.' Trust me, they take one look at this list and they won't want to listen to anything you say. You're attacking their competence."

"So what do I do?"

"Pick two, maybe three things that you could softly suggest. Only pick the ones that are the most important and could really help the company."

"I like them all," Andrea said, realizing she sounded a bit like a child at the ice cream shop.

"I know, and for what it's worth, they all seem valid. But the goal is to get them to agree to try."

Trying not to pout, Andrea asked, "So which ones do you think are most important?"

Without hesitating, Tyler said, "For Gretchen, her sales people need a good kick in the ass. Show her your commission idea and kibitz back and forth with her about the particulars until she is sold. And secondly, absolutely spend the money on the website to add an online ordering process. Maybe whoever does that for you can help with online advertising strategies as well."

"And Sammi?"

"You need to have good quality applicants in line, so if you need to do some more, you know, pruning of the deadwood, you've got good people to replace them. Have her revamp the introduction to the company and how she presents the jobs. You need a workforce that thinks for themselves in order to be nimble and quick. Identify the characteristics in the best workers and tell Sammi you're looking for that kind of person. And then for a second thing, talk about your new training."

"*My* new training? I didn't know I had *new* training yet."

"You have to. You have to bring in new hires and teach them all about how to work at Juggernaut. Explain the bonus program and why it is a good deal. Explain the delinking of reviews and raises. Teach them all about the team environment and then hurry up and start your video training program you talked about. I think that'd really help."

Andrea thought about all that Tyler said and countered, "So rip these pages up and keep it simple, huh?"

"No, don't rip them up. Save them for another day when you think they may be open to some more ideas."

"Got it. Thanks, Unc. I could've screwed everything up."

"Nah, you wouldn't. And hey, I learned something too."

Grinning back at him, she asked, "What's that?"

"Look at all these customers! I better start thinking about opening up for breakfast on the weekends."

MONDAY, APRIL 16

After ten work days, the total unit count sat at 1,879. Doing her math, it was easy to see they were about twenty-five units short of the pace they needed to make four thousand for the month. Apparently, Bentley could do the math as well.

Deep in thought, the knock on her open door startled Andrea. She looked up, and Bentley was standing at the threshold.

"Can I come in?"

"Of course. What can I do for you, sir?"

"I've seen your latest numbers. You aren't even halfway to four thousand yet. I don't think you're going to make it."

"We got off to a slower start than usual. It was my fault. I didn't give them the goal early enough to, you know, charge them up."

Bentley pondered that answer for a moment, then went a totally different direction. "You still hold the watch, right?" he asked, his eyes peering at her over his glasses.

"I do. What do you need done?"

"Tim's been buried in requests from the bank. They want to know what is going on with the bonuses we've been paying. He doesn't have time to explain it all, so I need you to write up a document that explains what's going on here in your department. Ten or fifteen pages of detail should do it."

Andrea gulped, then asked, "When do you need it?"

"Tomorrow morning by nine. Make sure you proofread, and the numbers have to match the P&L, so here is a copy."

"OK, I'll have it done," Andrea said, fighting the urge to comment on how unrealistic the request was.

Bentley started to get up, but sat down again. He had bags under his eyes and seemed less energetic than usual.

"Let me ask you a question, Ms. Lane," he said. "Do you ever worry about failing? I mean, you're off to a slow start this month, yet you seem unconcerned."

Caught off guard by the personal nature of the question, Andrea took a moment to gather her thoughts.

"Well, I certainly don't want to fail, but my uncle taught me that failure isn't a crime. It's not a sin. It's a step in learning. He taught me that the only real failure is in not trying at all. So I just give it everything I got, and if that isn't enough, well, then it's not enough. I'll learn from it."

Bentley stared back at her for a moment, then quietly said, "Damn expensive lesson."

"Only if I lose…sir."

WEDNESDAY, APRIL 18

Andrea met with Sammi on the 17th and found her very receptive to her suggestions for improving the "Meet and Greet" process for new hires and the training concepts as well. She particularly liked Andrea's one-page description of her idea of the ideal candidate to work in the Manufacturing Department.

Taking the confidence she gained from that into her meeting today with Gretchen helped her broach some uneasy topics.

"So what do you think about the structure of the commission here?" Andrea pointed to the document she had drawn up with the details of the commission formula.

"How did you think of this?" Gretchen asked.

"Well, I read some books on bonus programs and adapted the guidelines of an effective bonus plan to it. Commissions are essentially just bonuses, but they're almost easier because you can just take a percentage of the sales revenue. Do you think this could work for you?"

"Well, I'd like it if I were a salesperson, but some of the people might not feel that way. Honestly, Andi, I might not be suited well for this job. I can't motivate these people to do their best. If I could, you'd have to add another shift to cover all the work. I'm just not sure I'm a great sales *manager*."

Andrea took her time responding. Tyler had coached her. He'd reminded her to give time for the other VPs to think it out themselves. She recalled Tyler's words: *Don't feel pressured to comment on every random question or thought. If they are critical of one part of the plan, don't go on the defensive and immediately try to defend your thought. Just let it be. Ask other questions around it and sort of guide them toward coming up with a better answer or maybe realizing your plan was close to being on target.*

"Let me ask you this, Gretch. If one of your poor performing sales reps left today, have you got anybody in mind you could replace them with?"

"Not exactly. Most of the good ones out there all want more money."

"So, if you altered the pay structure to something close to this, could they make that kind of money?" Andrea tapped the one-page bonus plan summary.

Gretchen took a moment to peruse it and said, "Well, I-I don't know."

Andrea nodded. "Tough question. Suppose it was you. You've always been a dynamite sales person. Suppose you were working under this commission plan. Could you make big money?"

"Oh, jeez, yes! That's what kinda bothers me a bit. I mean, it almost pays too well for the person who could really produce. I woulda cleaned up if I had this one to work with."

Fighting every urge in her body, Andrea remained quiet, waiting for Gretchen's light bulb to go on.

Suddenly, her eyes widened and she said, "Hey! How bad would that be? So a rep makes a killing. We're not being over generous. The math works out. If he or she were really good, they'd bring in a ton of business and the company would win too. With this bonus structure, that's possible."

Andrea raised her eyebrows and played devil's advocate. "What about the reps who made less? And what about the problems you had in the past with commissions?"

"I'm just thinking, our old system was different. This one could work. And you know if reps are unhappy because it's too hard for them, well, maybe it's time for them to find a job they're better suited for."

Tyler, you're a friggin' genius. You said they'd figure it out themselves and you were—

Her thought was interrupted as Gretchen nearly bolted out of her seat. "Oh! Oh, damn! I just realized something."

"What?" Andrea asked.

Gretchen started to laugh, a strange glow of relief on her face.

"What if—oh yeah, what if I'm not a *bad* manager after all? What if the problem all along was the pay structure? I mean, you changed the line workers' pay structure and everybody complained and hated it, but now they're liking those big bonuses and production is higher than ever. Maybe it isn't *me*! Maybe I just didn't have the right structure in place to motivate everybody!"

Again, fighting the urge to stand up, raise her fist in the air, and shout *right on!* Andrea nodded her head and said, "Gretch, girl, I think you're onto something."

FRIDAY, APRIL 20

Every day for the last week, the supervisors had been actively joining their lines and helping to speed everything up. On Friday the 20th, Andrea rolled up her sleeves and joined them as well. At 3:52 p.m., Thomas bellowed out, "Two hundred!"

The lines were on fire. Everything moved smoothly and smiles were plastered on every face.

"There'll be jackets tonight!" one of the workers on Line 2 yelled out. Everyone cheered. There were still thirty-two employees without jackets, and they knew ten more would be snaring theirs this evening.

As Andrea worked on Line 3 with the Glimmer Stone installers, she stopped what she was doing and went over to Ji-woo Park, a three-year veteran of the line. She went to the end of the line and flipped the switch to turn off the engine. The line belt stopped immediately and everyone looked up.

"Line 3 has to stop for sixty seconds. Everybody else continue." Gazing out at the rest of workers on her line, she said, "OK, did you guys see that? Did you see what Ji-woo was doing?"

No one had any idea what she was talking about. Ji-woo looked up from his work, terrified.

"Let me show you quickly what he did. It was brilliant. It was perfect. Look here. While the belt was still moving, he applied the glue to the stone first and then the second one he held in his palm. He didn't need to pick up the vase and slow it down; he pasted these last two stones in on the fly. Ji-woo, you genius, this is what I'm talking about. This is what I want you to do. Find new ways to shave ten seconds off here and there, and when we do, we have to show everybody else so we build a process of best work practices. Ji-woo, we're going to film you doing that so everyone else can learn too. Great job, super job!"

Ji-woo stood there, sporting a Grand Canyon–sized grin.

Andrea looked around at everybody and nodded to Terry at the number one position to flick the switch and start the belt up again.

"OK, sorry, we lost a few seconds there, but it was worth it. Ji-woo, you just keep doing what you're doing!"

She finished the shift with her team on the line, and as they wrapped up the night, Thomas called out, "Two hundred and twenty-one!" Whoops and screams followed. It was the highest unit count they'd ever reached.

Andrea gave out ten more jackets and thanked everyone for a great week. The total on the board was now 2,859—a fraction above the pace to reach four thousand.

Andrea clapped along with everyone else and headed up the stairs to her office. She sat down at her desk and tried to come back to earth. A wide smile was pasted onto her face and she found she couldn't erase it.

A knock on the door snapped her out of her reverie.

"Robbie! Hey."

"Hey, yourself. Remember me?" he asked playfully.

"You work here, right?" Andrea said, playing along.

"Well, I collect a paycheck here. Some people would call that work. Some don't. I hear you've been busy going out to lunch and drinks and stuff with your new friends, Sammi and Gretchen."

"Ah, now I get it," Andrea said. "You're jealous. You're such a baby."

"That's me. I'm a hungry baby. Wanna go out for dinner with me? I could tell you all about how my life has changed since the last time we dined together."

"Wow, that was, what, five years ago?"

Robbie chuckled. "Feels like it. I'm buying."

"I'm getting my jacket."

WEDNESDAY, APRIL 25

The ten o'clock meeting with Andrea's supervisors was nearly finished. Each one had summarized their review and raise efforts during the month, and with only a few exceptions, most of the employees seemed to be getting used to the new reality. Most who received raises were loving it, and some who didn't felt left out. Satisfied that each supervisor was communicating well, Andrea asked if there were any questions.

Malik said, "Well, I think all of us were wondering what it was you did the other day. You know, shutting down Line 3 for a minute or so. I mean, we were racing the clock and we lost some time there. I'm not sure we get why what Ji-woo did was so important."

"It's a good question, Malik, and I meant to explain that. It was a bit dramatic and you certainly don't need to shut down the line every time someone does something good. But this is a very strong teaching tool that I want each of you to do more often."

Andrea paused to make sure she had their attention. "It's called 'catch somebody doing something right.' I didn't invent this. It's listed in a lot of good business books as a powerful teaching tool. The concept is that when you see something being done extremely well, or some new approach to a task that works better than usual, it's really effective to point it out to everyone right then and there.

"Now there were at least six or eight workers on Line 3 that could do exactly as Ji-woo did and save a ton of time. When you point it out like that, you give instant credit to the employee—a great atta boy in front of everyone else. And you make it clear to others that may not be sure what the best procedure is that this thing that you're pointing out is a good and approved technique. Now they all know it too, and if they weren't sure before, your remarks remove all doubt. This is best when doing a complicated task or a time-consuming task. Now if the others follow the same procedure, they save time too."

"But we don't necessarily have to stop the line, right?" Meghan asked.

"Right. I did that for effect. If you can demonstrate it again and not have to shut the belt off, go for it. Or maybe right after a break, before they start up again, have the employee demonstrate it one more time."

Reese nodded his head and said, "Got it. I like it. Great way to spotlight the employee's efforts too."

"Absolutely," Andrea added. "Now, we've got three and a half business days left before the end of the month. What's our unit count right now?"

Reese rose and stepped out of the office, onto the walkway. Looking down at the floor, he could see the board.

Sticking his head back into the room, he said, "We're at 3,324. We need seven hundred and twenty-six more by Monday night. It's gonna be close!"

"Well, let's get to work. We still have twelve more line workers without jackets, so we need a couple of two-hundred-unit days."

The supervisors filed out of the room, hustling to join their team on the line. Meghan and Reese were on the way down the hall as Malik reached the doorway.

"Malik, wait," Andrea called out.

Malik turned.

Andrea motioned him to shut the door and sit down. With a modest degree of trepidation, he did.

"Malik, I know you need to get down there but I had a quick question for you. Who is your number two in command?"

Scratching his head, Malik frowned and replied, "Well, I'm not sure. I haven't given it much thought."

"You should. But, hey, I wanted to tell you that I've noticed the morale on Lines 1 and 2 is high and your people seem very willing to talk to you and joke a bit. I like that. I think you're doing a great job, so effective retroactive back to the beginning of this pay period, I'm bumping you up by two hundred dollars a month. Thank you and keep it up."

Malik's face broke into a wide smile. "Thank you, Andrea! This is kinda funny isn't it?"

"How so?" Andrea asked, knowing the answer.

"You did the same thing to me that I'm doing to my line workers. And I fell for it. But aren't you forgetting something?"

Andrea smiled and shook her head. "Not at all. I wasn't done yet. Malik, if you'd like to make even more money, you need to identify who your number two is and get him or her trained to cover for you in a pinch. When that is done, we'll talk about money again."

Malik howled. "Hey, you're pretty good at this. I'm motivated to do it now."

"That's the idea, isn't it?" Andrea said. "Now, go on. Get out of here and get some work done."

"Yes, ma'am!" Malik gave a comical salute and headed out the door.

Andrea could hear him whistling all the way down the hall.

FRIDAY, APRIL 27

"That's number one hundred ninety-five," Thom McCann called out, and everyone cheered. It was only four o'clock and nothing short of a catastrophe would stop them from breaking two hundred.

It had been four days since they last topped two hundred and the employees without jackets were getting antsy. Meghan, Malik, and Reese were filling in for two who were sick and one on vacation, working the lines side-by-side with the employees.

Andrea watched them with pride and then returned to her office. For the eighth time this month, she poured over the payroll reports to convince herself that labor cost for the month would be under the 28-percent goal. She'd done all she could to reduce overtime, and with the exception of Dale's repair hours, she felt it was under control. Dale had some extra work to do for Tim, rewiring his computer system, and he showed over fourteen OT hours already.

"Two hundred!!" Thomas screamed out on the PA system. His amplified voice was incredibly loud, but the resulting cheer was louder.

Andrea smiled to herself. *There'll be jackets handed out tonight!*

When the horn sounded at five o'clock, Thomas competed against it, shouting out, "Two hundred and sixteen!"

It wasn't their record, but it was a very fine day.

Andrea made a show of walking down the stairs with two large bags in each hand. She stopped on the fifth step as usual and placed two bags on either side of her.

"Who's got the hat?" she asked.

Reese brought up a baseball cap with all the names in it. Slyly, Andrea pulled something out of her pocket and surreptitiously slipped it into the hat as well.

She stared out at everyone and waited for the noise level to die down. "All right! Let's see who gets a jacket today."

She pulled the first white slip out of the hat, read it, and called out, "Ginny Yates!"

The diminutive, fifty-something veteran of Line 1 walked up proudly and said, "I think I'll take a small."

Andrea withdrew a small size and handed it to Malik. As was the custom, he helped her put it on, and she pranced around dramatically, showing it off like a fashion model. Everyone laughed.

Andrea continued pulling out the next nine names and everyone applauded. The two remaining employees who did not have a jacket yet clapped as well, but their smiles were a little more forced.

Andrea said, "I got two more names in here, and I say it's time to break the rules and give them out." She looked at the two men, standing side-by-side, and said, "Lance, Jaylen, come on up and get your jackets."

The two stragglers happily strode up and claimed their prize. They bowed repeatedly and the audience howled.

Andrea looked back in the hat and said, "Hey, wait a minute. What's this?"

She pulled out a yellow slip of paper and said, "This one says *Malik* on it. Must be some mistake. We don't want a slacker like him to get a jacket, do we?"

Again everyone laughed, and a couple voices called out, "Give it to him!"

Andrea removed an extra-large size and helped the tall man to put it on.

Malik, his bright white teeth contrasting with his dark black skin, could be seen smiling broadly way in the back of the room.

Andrea went through the same routine with Meghan and Reese. Everyone applauded, and it was over by 5:20.

Still standing on the fifth step, she called out, "We hit 3,872 today! One day left in the month. We need a hundred and seventy-eight more. Have a great weekend and, on Monday, let's do what everyone said we couldn't do! Good night."

She returned to her office and wiped a tear from her eyes.

That was fun. No matter what happens, tonight made it all worthwhile. Win or lose now, that was one special moment tonight, and I don't think I'll ever forget it.

MONDAY, APRIL 30

Tim sat in Craig's office and made himself comfortable in the deep leather chair. He had his 7:00 a.m. cup of coffee and he was glad to be able to start his day this way.

"Sandra, Tim and I have a lot to go over," Craig said into the intercom. "I don't want any interruptions."

"Yes, sir. No one will be bothering you."

Craig leaned back in his chair and asked, "You been working on our little plan?"

"All weekend."

Craig smiled and said, "Bring me up to date."

"Well, first of all, I had the repair guy run up a bunch of OT hours rewiring my office, and when he was done, I told him I changed my mind and wanted it done a different way. He put in another twenty hours this weekend."

Craig chuckled. "That's so devious, I love it. But one man's OT hours is not going to be enough to skewer the whole department's labor cost."

"No, but it's a good start. I also told—um, what's his name? Darnel, no, wait, I think it's Darrell, the repair guy—I told him he could come in to work late on Monday—10:00 a.m., but I'd clock him in at eight. He seemed to like the idea of sleeping in."

"How is that going to help?" Craig asked.

"I got a man inside the department who thinks as we do. You know, that all these changes in Manufacturing are crazy. Of course,

163

it helps that I spiff him a few fifties now and then so that he keeps agreeing with us. He removed a key part from the Line 1 mechanism after shutdown on Friday. With that whole line down for two hours, and another hour or more to install a new motor, there's no way they'll get to four thousand."

"Nice. Who's your man inside?" Craig asked.

"Probably best you don't know. Plausible deniability and all that," Tim said with a brief smirk.

"Say no more," Craig agreed. "What about the books?"

"I'm still cookin'. I got Bentley to sign off on writing off bad debt quarterly instead of yearly. We'll bury those costs in the April P&L. The bank will understand, but ole Bentley, he'll freak out 'cuz he only looks at the bottom line. Hell, he barely understands it all anyway."

Craig nodded. "Good. It's all coming together. By June or July, he'll be ready to sell and you and I'll get the whole company for a song. All we have to do now is make sure that Andrea doesn't screw it all up for us. We make sure she misses her goals and Bentley will fire her this week. I'm tired of her already."

The CFO rose from his seat and said, "Craig, I'm with you. I'll pull the P&L for April together within two days and send it to the bank. I'll conveniently forget to include Andrea's twelve-page diatribe explaining the math on the damn bonus program. Next, we'll meet with Bentley, and then she'll be out of our hair. Gotta get back to work now. See you at lunch."

Tim left the room as Craig remained seated, drumming his fingers on his desktop and asking himself if he'd done all he could do.

Andrea stepped into her office at 7:30, already in a good mood, anticipating the breakthrough four thousandth unit today. Knowing she had set the goal higher at 4,050 made her feel even more secure.

As the crew started showing up, Andrea went down to the floor and chatted them up. Doing her best to keep everyone relaxed and at their best, she made no mention of the goal that lay ahead.

Seeing Carol walking over to her usual Position 9 on the line, Andrea went up to her and gave her a hug. "Hey, short-timer, another month over already. How much longer before retirement day?"

Carol laughed at the moniker Andrea gave her and replied, "Four more months. Although I've gotta tell ya, it's been kinda fun around here lately. I'm going to miss it."

"You could withdraw your papers and stay," Andrea suggested.

Carol laughed and replied, "I'm not gonna miss it that much!"

Andrea nodded and laughed as well.

The horn sounded and all six of the Position 1 workers headed to their post to flip the switch and start the belt motors for each line. Lines 2 through 6 started up flawlessly, but Line 1 gave a brief buzz and did nothing.

Andrea's eyes went wide and she called out to Malik, "What's the issue?"

Malik looked it over and signaled Andrea to come and see for herself.

As she arrived, Malik quietly said, "It looks like it's been tampered with."

"Oh, jeez! Call Dale right away. This is not a good day for a line to go down."

The next hour was a madhouse on the floor. Dale was not in the building and calls to his home went unanswered. Malik was busy combining Lines 1 and 2, but the results were ugly. He moved some of the functions back to Line 1 and they manually pushed and carried the items up the line. Workers from Lines 3 and 4 tried to help, but it had little effect—too many people trying to function in too small an area.

Meanwhile, Lines 3 through 6 had nothing to do but finish up the few remaining straggler items left on the lines at closing time Friday night. By 9:00 a.m. the team had only finished producing seven units and were well behind.

At 9:10, Andrea spotted Dale looking askance at his timecard and punching in at the clock. She raced over to him and called out, mid-run, "Dale, you're late. We had a breakdown on Line 1."

Visibly upset, Dale headed to the line and asked, "What happened?"

"Not sure," Andrea said. Then as she got closer to him, she whispered, "Looks like someone messed with it."

Five seconds later, after no more than a cursory look, Dale agreed, "No shit. They opened up the shell and pulled the wires out, and the reel too."

"Do you have those parts?" Andrea asked, thinking to herself that her career depended on his answer.

"No. I mean, we just buy the whole motor assembly in one piece. I don't actually have the wires and the reel."

Andrea looked up at the ceiling and composed herself. "Can you just replace the whole motor?"

"Well, yeah, but there's a lot to do. It'll take me ninety minutes or so."

"We don't have ninety minutes, Dale," Andrea said as quietly as she could.

Dale stood there for a minute, thinking. "Andrea, I can fix this quick. I'll cannibalize Line 6's motor and install the parts here. Line 6 can't do much of anything now anyway. Then I'll install a new motor on Line 6 so you can get going here, where you really need it. I'll have Line 1 back up in twenty minutes."

Andrea wanted to kiss him, but merely flashed a smile at him and said, "Go for it!"

Twenty-eight minutes later, Line 1 was back up and running, but the crew had lost over an hour and a half of productive worktime.

Andrea walked over to the stairway and yelled out, "OK, we're up. And I've got some news for you. The real goal for this month is four thousand. I told all of you it was 4,050 so we could blow out the goal that the rest of management was sure we couldn't reach. We've got six hours left to do one hundred and twenty-one more units. And I'm going to change my goal too. If we can reach 4,050,

I'll give you each a crisp one-hundred-dollar bill *tonight*. So, let's rock and roll!"

Her announcement was greeted with stunned silence, then followed by some whoops and hollers. The race was on.

At noon, Craig and Tim headed out of the building for lunch. They walked a block and a half to a hotel restaurant and waited until they had ordered to start talking business.

"What the hell happened? She got the line back up by 9:50."

"That little pecker, the repair guy, he waltzed in at nine o'clock. I told him to sleep in and come in at ten. I mean, really, when was the last time someone came in early when they didn't have to?"

Ignoring the rhetorical question, Craig asked, "How did he get it up and going so fast?"

"Damn kid. He's pretty smart. He stole the parts he needed out of the Line 6 motor and got Line 1 back up quickly. Then he spent the time to fix Line 6 while the rest of the lines caught up. Pretty shrewd."

"Yeah it was. Something you should have thought of, Tim."

"I'm the CFO, not a mechanic. What have *you* done to help us lately?"

"I've prepped the bank, remember. I've schmoozed 'em, bought them lunches and dinners, and convinced them that you and I know what we're doing and once we're in charge, the company will be profitable again."

Tim thought about that and nodded. Then, rethinking it, tentatively asked, "Will it?"

"Will it what?"

"Be profitable again."

Craig shook his head. "It doesn't matter. With Bentley gone, we pay ourselves the big bucks and drain this puppy dry as long as the funds hold out. We'll slash and burn, cut payroll, and get by as long as we can, and meanwhile, we'll pull out enough to pad our retirement funds ten times more than we have now. When the bank decides they won't loan us any more money, we close the doors and walk away clean."

Tim smiled. "Leave the bank and employees holding the bag."

"Exactly. Only the smart win. That's us. Everybody else gets what they deserve."

Something happened at Juggernaut Enterprises that hadn't occurred since the company was seven months old. The employees voluntarily cut their lunches short and returned to their spots on the line. Everyone seemed intent on producing enough units to reach the goal.

At 2:57 in the afternoon, Thomas McCann bellowed out, "Fourrrrr thouuuusand!"

Everyone cheered.

Andrea, her hair falling down around her face, her brow sweaty, grease stains on her skirt and blouse, looked up at the board and gave a cheer. So did nearly everyone else. She looked around the room and yelled out, "Way to go! Come on, let's not slow down now. Fifty more and you get an extra hundred. Let's show them what we can do!"

She smiled at the crew, and for a fraction of an instant, she again caught Stan's eye and noticed he was looking at her with an odd expression on his face. Not angry, not sad, not grinning like a madman. Just mouth open, as though he were astonished at the sight of her.

She shook that off and returned to her role on Line 2. Every few minutes, Thomas would call out the new total for the month. At four thirty, he said, "Four thousand and forty."

Again, Andrea cheered and called out, "We can do it. Ten more! That's all you need!"

Going as hard as she'd ever worked before, she pushed the product through, finally leaving Line 2 and joining Line 6, which was down a man.

"Come on! We can do this," she cheerleaded for everyone to hear.

Thomas called out each one as it happened. "Four thousand forty-seven!" he said.

Andrea, totally caught up in the moment, hustled all the more, constantly egging the crew on. Suddenly she caught several of the people on Line 6 staring at her, doing nothing.

"What's wrong? We have almost four minutes left before the horn. We're practically there."

She straightened up and gazed around the room. Everyone had slowed down or stopped completely.

Carol called out to her, "Andrea, I think we did enough. We're all tired."

"I know. And all of you did great! I'm so proud of you, but I want you to get the extra bonus. Just three more and they're here on Line 6 already. I've got the hundreds here with me. We're almost done!"

A woman on Line 5 said, "Andrea, you've done enough. You don't have to pay out over $9,000 of your *own* money to say thank you. You say it every day to us when you work by our side. I think 4,047 is high enough. What do the rest of you think?"

Everyone had already stopped what they were doing and ceased working.

For the next two minutes there was a lot of murmuring going on and people talking among themselves.

Finally, speaking loudly enough to be heard over the din, Stan called out, "Enough, we did it! Let's knock off for the day." The horn blew fifteen seconds later.

Andrea hugged everyone on Line 6 and anyone else who was nearby and not afraid to get a grease smudge on their clothes.

Heading back to her upstairs office, she paused midway up the stairs and noticed no one had left yet. She stared at them and said, "You are the finest crew I've ever worked with. I will fight for you every day of the week. I love you guys. Now go home and relax. We'll see you all tomorrow."

As she turned to leave, one of the workers yelled out, "Thanks, Andrea. Don't forget: we need a May goal."

Andrea looked back and laughed as tears ran down her face. "You'll have it."

WEDNESDAY, MAY 2

t four that afternoon, Tim entered Bentley's office with a copy of the P&L for April in his hands. He wasted no time getting to the point.

"Sir, I'm afraid I have some bad news."

"What is it?" Bentley asked.

"We're showing a loss for April. With all the extra labor cost that Manufacturing is running, the company is in the red by sixteen thousand dollars." Tim delivered the news exactly as he had rehearsed it. Silently, he congratulated himself for effectively wording the news so Bentley would focus on Andrea's department and not on the paper losses caused by the quarterly bad debt and adjustments.

Tim seated himself while he observed Bentley going through the motions of looking over the P&L and pretending to understand each line entry. Tim purposely did not include the report that compared actual numbers to the forecasted numbers. Where he made changes would be too obvious then.

"She paid out a monster bonus of over $52,000 for the April work. That shows up in the accrued payroll costs. I dare say, she's done a lot of damage to our chances with the bank."

Bentley looked up at his CFO and nodded. "I'll be putting an end to that. Tonight!"

His mission accomplished, Tim rose from his seat and said, "I'm very sorry to have to bring you this news, sir. I wish I didn't have to. You certainly deserve better than this."

He turned to leave and mused to himself, *Actually, you don't deserve better. You're an old fool and you know nothing about running a business.*

Andrea sat at her desk, engaging in a guilty pleasure—in her head, she was replaying the noon meeting with the employees where she presented two bonus plans and told them they could select the one they liked best.

The first one was challenging but very doable and the bonus amount was generally a bit less than the amount they received for April's effort. The second one was much more aggressive, returning much higher payouts for every unit completed over two hundred each day. It returned a bonus nearly 10 percent higher than April.

After considerable discussion, the employees voted for the second plan, just as Andrea had hoped. Now, enjoying her reverie, she remembered the most important aspect of the meeting: the confidence everyone displayed as they discussed breaking two hundred nearly every day. The goal for the twenty-two-day month was set at 4,250. If they made it, it would be the most productive month in company history.

And I'll be around to see it because we produced over four thousand units and held labor cost to 25.5 percent. That thought produced a satisfied smile on her face.

Her reverie was interrupted by a voice on the intercom. It was Bentley's secretary asking her to come to his office immediately.

Andrea stared out the window at the evening's darkness. The Juggernaut Building was empty except for the janitorial crew and the evening guard. She had been standing there for fifteen minutes, saying nothing and trying hard to think nothing as well.

Finally, she turned and walked back to her desk. Picking up her cell phone, she dialed the Professor's Bar and Grill. Uncle Tyler answered on the first ring.

"You working tonight?" she asked.

"I'm here, but others are doing most of the work. I'm just mingling and, you know, doing quality control tests on some new beer that came in."

Even now, her uncle could get a small smile from her.

"Would it be OK if I came by so we could talk for a bit?"

Tyler agreed quickly, and she showed up twenty minutes later.

They sat in a dark corner booth, and she didn't have to tell him what happened. He could read it on her face.

"He fired you, didn't he?"

"I thought he was calling me in to congratulate me. We produced 4,047 units and labor cost, by my calculation, was 25.5 percent. I made both the targets that I promised, but he said labor cost was higher and it didn't matter because he's not happy and that was part of the deal. And he's not happy because the company lost money in April and he blames me. He's fixated on the $52,000 in bonus money—no matter how many times I tell him that only about $22,000 of that was actually extra and when you factor in the higher productivity…well, you know the rest. I don't think he's the sharpest tool in the shed."

Tyler sat quietly, waiting. He knew that there was more to come.

She took a sip of her Chardonnay and locked eyes with her uncle. "I told him he was crazy. I yelled at him and told him that what we were doing was exactly what the bank would want to see. I went on and on. I'm sort of embarrassed now, thinking about it."

"I like it so far," Tyler replied. "What else did you say?"

"I told him he ordered us to be creative, to come up with ways to save the company, and I was virtually the only one doing anything. I told him he ought to be giving me a raise and more responsibility, not firing my ass. Aw, jeez, I droned on for too long. Finally, I told him that I worked for cheap because I gave a damn and I guess that was the wrong thing to do at his company. Then I walked out. I'll have to go back and pick my things up tomorrow."

She stopped talking and started to take a sip of wine, but she put the glass back down and started to cry silently. She wiped at her eyes with the napkin and shook her head. "Unc, I loved that job. I don't want to be fired. I was just getting warmed up. I've been in this industry for most of my adult life. What am I going to do now?"

Tyler took another swig of beer, and in a calm, quiet voice, he said, "Andi, the skills you have and the lessons you learned are invaluable. And they're transferable to any industry. What you've become, practically right before my eyes, is a damn good people manager. You understand human nature better; you've been through a war, you've gained insights that only come from actual experience, and you've had a truckload of all that in the last three months. I think you can go anywhere you want with the skills you now have."

Andrea looked at her uncle and flashed him a smile. "You oughta be in sales, Unc."

"We're all in sales, honey. Every last one of us. The difference is some folks don't realize that."

Her tears stopped falling as she headed home to get a good night's sleep.

FRIDAY, MAY 4

Andrea used sick time to take a day off, returning to work on the 4th at eight o'clock. She wasted no time letting the supervisors know there would be a short meeting in her office at 9:00 a.m.

With that time set, she took a long stroll to the warehouse and spotted Robbie helping an employee crate some patio furniture. She waved, got his attention, and met him at his office door. He led her in and said, "I heard what happened. It…it totally sucks."

She shook her head. "I know. I'm just here today to pick up my things and turn in my keys."

Robbie froze. "I don't get it. I thought you made your goals. Over four thousand units and wasn't labor cost under the target too?"

"By my calculations it was. But the company lost money last month and he blames it on the bonus that I paid the manufacturing team. I argued with him, but he's the boss so he can do what he wants."

Robbie sat down in his chair and stared at the ceiling. "You were doing some really good things. He can't see it. I suspect Tim helped him to interpret the reasons for the loss."

"Oh, I don't think he'd—"

"He would," Robbie said, cutting her off.

Andrea looked at him, her wheels turning.

"Robbie, do you know something I don't know?"

Robbie cleared his throat. "I, uh, I had a run in with him a few years back. He showed his true colors. I won't bore you with all the details, but he's very good at pointing the finger at someone else when he might be the culprit himself. I don't trust him, and you shouldn't either."

Andrea sat down as well, pondering that. After they talked for a few more minutes about the direction the company might go in now, Andrea checked her watch, stood back up, and said, "I've gotta go. I'm going to stop by and tell Sammi and Gretchen, then I'm meeting with my supervisors for one last time."

Robbie nodded. Their eyes locked for a second and he said, "Whether you work here or not, I still like going out to dinner with you and, well, I'd like to get to know you better. If, you know, that's something you, um, might—"

"It is!" Andrea said. "I-I'd like that. You can still tell me all about Juggernaut and I can tell you what it's like, you know, to be unemployed." She tried to chuckle but wasn't sure it was all that funny.

"You make it sound so appealing," Robbie said, a smirk on his face. "On second thought, going out is expensive—I may have to cook you a Top Ramen Surprise dinner instead. I might be unemployed along with you in a few months."

He came over and gave her a hug. She hung on for a delicious moment too long and left without looking back.

Her stops at the Sales and Marketing Department and HR were brief and to the point. Both Gretchen and Sammi looked defeated as she left.

At nine o'clock, the three supervisors filed into her office.

With the supervisors unaware of yesterday's events, Meghan jumped right in and said, "Lots of smiling faces today at work. Everybody got their check or pay stub and saw those hefty bonuses on them."

Andrea grinned. "That was going to be my first question today, but I saw them too and, well, I definitely wanted to be here to see that."

Continuing, she added, "First of all, I want to congratulate all three of you on an outstanding effort in April. I don't think I've ever seen anybody work so hard."

She paused for a moment to let them enjoy the happier moment. Then she continued, "Unfortunately, Bentley is not happy with the results. The company lost money last month and he blames the high bonus amount. Today is my last day here."

Andrea wanted to keep going but verbalizing that thought choked her up.

"You're kidding! He fired you?" Meghan asked.

"It's his company. I plan to recommend to him that Malik succeed me since he is the most experienced of you. I doubt my recommendation will mean much to him, I'm sorry, but at least I'd know the employees are in good hands if he picks any of you. I suspect, however, that Craig Saunders will just take on my duties."

"This sucks, Andrea," Malik said. Reese seconded it.

"We were just starting to mesh as a team," Meghan said. "It's really not fair."

"Well, we know how that is," Andrea replied. "Life isn't fair. All you can do is move on."

The three supervisors looked at each other and shook their heads.

Andrea wanted to wrap it up before she fell apart in front of them. "I'm going to take ten minutes to gather up my personal things and then I'm going to Bentley's office to turn in my keys. I-I want to say it's been an honor to work with you three fine people, and I will miss you greatly." Her voice cracked slightly on the last sentence, but she didn't waver.

She came around her desk and hugged each of them and told them not to say anything to the employees until she was out of the building. They agreed and left the office.

Andrea looked around. Very few of the items in the office were actually hers. A small picture on the wall, a Magic Eight Ball paperweight, two favorite pens, and her laptop. It only took two minutes to pack them up.

Nostalgically, she took one last look around the room. Needing to linger a few minutes more, she remembered the feeling she had last Monday night after they had reached 4,047 units produced—a highlight worth remembering.

She pictured the scene that she looked out over as she was ascending the stairs. She replayed the moment in her mind. *I stood there and said, 'You are the finest crew I've ever worked with. I will fight for you every day of the week. I love you guys. Now go home and—'*

"Wait a minute!" Andrea said out loud.

Still mumbling to herself she said, "I said I'd fight for them. Every day of the week! What am I doing? They're counting on me. This is bullshit. I'll just cut a new deal. I'm not giving up yet!"

Leaving her belongings in a box on her desk, she marched down the hall to Bentley's office. She walked in and asked his secretary, "Is he in?"

"Yes, I'll let him know you—"

"No need," Andrea said as she blasted past her and pushed Bentley's door open.

"Mr. Bentley, I was supposed to bring you my keys today and leave, but I don't want to."

"Uh, um, excuse me? You can't come barging in here like that!"

"What are you gonna do? Fire me? You did that already, and I just accepted it. Listen, I'm on your side. I care about this company. I've turned a bored, disengaged set of employees into a fired up, enthusiastic team that is capable of increasing productivity every week. This is a key part of the solution you're looking for, and I want to stay here and help you turn this ship around. Let's consider the decisions made yesterday to be part of an *ongoing* discussion. Maybe you will fire me someday, but let's not make it now. Give me another few months. Keep me until July when we hear from the bank again. I'll give you four thousand units every month with lower and lower labor cost. Let me help you."

The words poured out of her in a torrent, and she paused to catch her breath.

"Ms. Lane, I appreciate that you care so much. I will say, you-you are a very energetic manager and I admire your fearless devotion to the job. But I—"

Hearing the clamor all the way down the hall, Craig and Tim hurriedly entered the room and immediately focused their attention on Bentley.

"Sir, don't listen to her," Craig said. "She is the cause of the problems. You made a good decision yesterday to fire her, and I want to remind you that this is no time to show indecision. The bankers have already been notified that you are taking hard action to penalize senior managers who are underperforming."

Tim tag-teamed him. "Also, sir, we have informed the bank that Craig himself will slide over and run the Manufacturing Department, immediately ending this bonus nonsense and saving the company thousands of bonus dollars plus Ms. Lane's salary. We can show that with Craig working for the same amount he makes now, you can save the company over a hundred thousand dollars a year in pay and benefits. That will impress them."

"Well, I-I have to admit, that sounds good. I—"

As though it were becoming the national pastime, Andrea interrupted again. "Mr. Bentley, give me ten minutes with the bankers and I will shoot that argument so full of holes it'll look like breakfast at the Cheerios factory. Our bonus program did *not* cause the losses. If the accounting had been done right, all the product we created would still either be on the books as inventory or out the door as sales. Since our labor cost was less than normal, you should be seeing higher total labor cost but far higher total sales."

"Excuse me," Craig interrupted again. "It doesn't matter what she says. We've informed the bank already and they were very happy with the changes. We can win over the bank just fine without her so-called help. Sir, you have to put your foot down and dismiss her once and for all."

An eerie silence filled the room as everyone waited for Bentley to make the decision.

Finally, he took a deep breath and said, "Craig is right. Ms. Lane, your employment is terminated. Please leave the premises and—"

"Not so fast!" Robbie said, entering the room and cutting off Bentley again, midsentence.

"What are you doing here?" Craig asked.

"I'm here to turn in my resignation too. If she goes, I go," Robbie said.

"Me too!" Sammi called out as she entered Bentley's office.

"I'm gone also," Gretchen added. "And just for good measure, we're going to need everyone to step forward a bit so others can come on in and turn in their keys. They all quit too."

Meghan, Malik, and Reese entered the room holding up their keys and fobs.

"We don't want to work for anybody else," Meghan said. "If you fire Andrea and go back to the old pay model and all the old procedures that really never worked, well, we'd all fail anyway."

Craig and Tim looked like twins with their mouths stuck open. The brief moment of silence was broken when Bentley's secretary screamed out, "You can't all come in here!"

Malik smiled. "That'd be just about everybody else." Peering out Bentley's office door, he spotted the workers' leader and said, "Stan, you want to tell 'em?"

In his overalls, Stan stepped into Bentley's office for the first time. Every eye in the room turned to him.

He gazed around and said, "I'm not exactly a big fan of management. But I'll tell you one thing. Andrea works hard and she gives a damn, which is more than I can say about some of you. Now, I don't agree with everything she's done, but she's kept her word and we are all making more money now, and I tell ya, we are a well-oiled machine. You get rid of her and take away our bonus program and our supervisors, well, we're all going to want more money and you won't be seeing any more four-thousand-unit months. We've got rights, and I'm warning you, you fire the only person who treats us like real people and this place will go to hell in a handbasket."

Again, silence reigned.

Clearing his throat, Bentley said in a quieter voice, "This is all very disconcerting. I think—I think under the circumstances, we should just go back to work and—and Craig, you and Andrea work out your differences. I think it's best not to rock the boat right now with management changes. The bank will have to get over it."

Andrea beamed. Craig and Tim rolled their eyes. Everyone else cheered.

SATURDAY, MAY 5

Andrea showed up early for her Saturday morning breakfast with her uncle.

"Well, well! If it isn't the conquering hero," Tyler said.

"Make all the jokes you want, but I'm still employed. What a day yesterday was!"

Anxious to hear the whole story, Tyler hurriedly set the table and served two plates of food.

"Wait just a second," Tyler said as he unfolded his napkin, placed it on his lap, and picked up his fork. "I want to be ready to start stuffing my face while you prattle on and on about your stirring victory."

Andrea laughed and began relating the story, nearly minute by minute, to her uncle. She went on for twenty minutes, nibbling at her breakfast as she spoke. Finally, she wrapped it up. "And then when Stan came in and spoke for the whole work crew, well, Bentley just kinda caved. He told Craig and me that we'd have to work out our differences and said he didn't want to rock the boat with managerial changes now. So I guess I'm in for the duration."

"Perfect timing. I just took my last bite," Tyler said.

"Glad I could accommodate," Andrea replied, chuckling.

Tyler shook his head. "Incredible story. I mean, you told your supervisors not to say anything until you were out of the building. But they must have told everyone anyway."

"I never got the whole story on that," Andrca said. "It might have been Robbie, Gretchen, or Sammi that spread the word. Anyway, it was very moving that they cared that much to offer to quit along with me."

"You know why they did, don't you?"

Andrea looked down at her plate in thought. "They like me?" she asked, not sure she believed it either.

Tyler shook his head. "Well, sure, they like you. And, if you don't mind me saying, it sounds to me like Robbie may have done it because he *really* likes you. But I don't think the others offered to quit just because they like you."

"What then?"

Tyler finished off his coffee and continued, "I think they liked what you were doing. Sammi and Gretchen are followers. They need someone to lead them, and you were filling that void. With you there, they liked the company's chances of turning things around. With you gone, they might as well quit too, because they saw the company going down.

"The three supervisors liked the new systems and knew that would end abruptly under Craig. They'd had a taste of the power of enlightened self-interest and didn't want to go backward.

"And the workers, they liked what you did for their bank accounts. They aren't willing to quit, but they're not beyond threatening a slowdown.

"Your actions, Andi, were the catalyst for all those things to happen. And now, oh…" Tyler stopped talking as he chuckled. "Oh, now, you, my dear, have been given the greatest opportunity of your life."

Wide-eyed, Andrea asked, "What do you mean?"

"Andi, Bentley just gave you the green light."

Andrea eyed her uncle, trying to fathom his meaning.

"Unc, I'm not playing baseball here. It's not second base I'm trying to steal."

Tyler's lips turned up into a secret smile. "The green light isn't just a baseball analogy. Now and then in life, you get the green light flashed at you for just a brief moment, and you have to move quickly to take advantage of it. This is your moment, Andi. When Bentley caved, without fully understanding what he was doing, he gave you that green light. Right now, for a short time, you can do just about anything you want and he won't fight you. Now! Now is when you have to continue making wholesale changes. You've got two months before the bank is going to review everything and make a final decision on loaning more money. Now, you have to kick it into gear and move faster than you ever have."

"You think I should steal second base?"

"Honey, you're already on second base. You've got the green light to steal third and then score."

Andrea took a bite of her breakfast and another long sip of coffee. Staring back at her uncle, she asked, "My guess is you have a few suggestions."

Tyler's face lit up. "Oh, baby, do I."

For the next hour, Tyler and Andrea discussed the next steps she had to put into motion. She suggested a few of her own and Tyler agreed she would be well on her way to third base if she could do them all by the end of June.

They finished their last cup of coffee, and Andrea gave her uncle a heartfelt hug.

"Having someone to talk this all out with has really helped me, Unc. Thanks!"

"You're doing the work, honey. I'm just on the sidelines where it's safe. You're the one calling the plays, taking the hits, and making it happen. Keep it up."

Andrea put her coat on and headed for the door.

As she reached it, Tyler called out to her, "And by the way, that was some turnaround by Stan. When I told you to try to win hearts and minds, I didn't really think you'd win him over too."

Andrea looked back and smiled broadly. "I vanquish my enemies when I make them my friends."

Tyler laughed. "That's a good one. Now, remember, the green light doesn't stay on forever. No dawdling." Then, as an afterthought, he added, "And I'll match your Lincoln quote with another from old Abe. He said, 'Things may come to those who wait, but only the things left by those who hustle.'"

"Message received, Unc!" Andrea called out over her shoulder.

As she walked down the street, she thought about the brief green light she had been given. *Pedal to the metal, girl. Time to get into the express lane.*

WEDNESDAY, MAY 9

The four of them were seated at Brannigan's and their orders had just been served to their table. Malik, Meghan, Reese, and Andrea were in one of the semicircle booths so they could hear each other easily but still have privacy from peering eyes and overreaching ears.

"All right, enough chit chat. We're here for two reasons—"

"To eat and get drunk?" Meghan asked, chuckling.

Andrea shook her head. "Who hired you?"

"You did, back when you were a supervisor."

Andrea looked at Reese and Malik and said, "You two must be a bad influence on her. She was quiet and reserved when I hired her."

Again Andrea shook her head and chuckled. "OK, back to work. We're here for two reasons: to celebrate a herculean effort by you three in April and to discuss our new initiatives in May.

"So," she said, raising her beer schooner up in the air in salute, "here's to you three for all you've done."

"How about a toast to us four?" Malik countered.

"I'll drink to that," Meghan and Reese said at nearly the same time.

Meghan elbowed Reese and said, "Try to name anything you won't drink to, Reese."

"I draw the line at, um, you know, nuclear war and stuff like that."

"A man of principle!" Meghan replied.

They finished their toast and Andrea started in again, "OK, the celebration part is over. I want to talk to you about a new initiative I want to start in May and get your input on this one."

Countering her new image as a party girl, Meghan immediately pulled out a notepad and prepared to write.

"Now, I have several we'll be discussing over the next few weeks, but here is the first initiative," Andrea said. "I want to develop more programs for training and education of supervisors *and* the line workers. I want us to learn how to motivate and engage the workers more and then apply what we learn to be more effective people managers."

"Learning things like 'catch someone doing something right' type things?" Malik asked.

"Exactly. Basic techniques that you can start applying right away."

"Like what?" Meghan asked.

"Well, I'm glad you asked," Andrea said, smiling. "I just happen to have one simple and important issue for you that I can share right now. In five minutes, I'm going to teach you the secret to being perceived as a positive manager of people. Are you ready?"

The three supervisors gave her a nod.

"The secret is…be more positive more often."

The look of disappointment on the supervisors' faces wasn't hard to read.

"OK, I know, too obvious. Doesn't sound like a secret, but here's the deal—multiple studies have been done on this topic and they've all come to generally the same conclusion. A very negative people manager constantly harps on what the employees are doing wrong. They yell at and berate the employees nearly all the time, then they express surprise when the employees become less responsive and fail to learn from their mistakes."

Reese butted in. "I think we all kinda know that, Andrea."

"I know you do. But what you probably don't know is *how* positive you need to be. The studies on this topic show that employees are far more responsive and far more engaged with their work when they perceive the manager to be a 'positive' manager." Andrea used her fingers to put air quotation marks around the word *positive*.

"So?" Reese asked, dragging the single syllable word out as long as he could.

Andrea finished his question for him. "So…what do you have to do to be *perceived* as positive? That is the secret that the studies revealed. To be perceived as positive, you have to have a ratio of a minimum of five-to-one positive to negative interactions. Some studies said as much as ten to one. Most however agree that five or six positive interactions for every one negative interaction is probably the right number."

"And a negative interaction is what, exactly?" Meghan asked as she took notes.

"A negative interaction," Andrea answered, "is any discussion you have with them about correcting an error or offering any form of criticism."

"But we're kinda avoiding that by, you know, doing the coaching about how they can get to the next pay level, aren't we?" Reese asked.

"Yes! Absolutely!" agreed Andrea. "But even when you're coaching, you are still essentially telling them what they are doing wrong or not perfectly right. Even the slightest critical comment puts that conversation into the negative category. Although, if you precede it with praise for what they are doing right, it lessens the blow so much that it minimizes the negative portion."

Malik shook his head. "I can tell you, they didn't do that shit in the military. Everything was, um, strongly worded, and they didn't waste any time trying to be nice."

"I think," Andrea said, "the military objective is to hurry up and get you up to speed so that you don't get killed. That's a whole different scenario, and I'm not sure it applies to our situation."

"Andrea, no offense, but it sounds a little like overkill," Reese said. "I mean, I think it comes off a bit phony to keep trying to praise people all the time and tell them how wonderful they are, especially if, you know, they're kinda average."

"Oh, of course, good point, Reese," Andrea replied. "That *would* sound phony. I'm not saying that a positive interaction has to include praise. Honestly, in my view, a positive interaction is any conversation you have with an individual employee about, well, anything that is not negative."

"I'm still not getting it," Meghan jumped in. "Like what?"

"Well, how was traffic this morning when you came in? I heard there was an accident on Highway 46."

Meghan stared at her, trying to fathom what that had to do with her question. "It was OK, but about my—"

"Meghan," Andrea interrupted. "*Any* conversation can be a positive interaction. What you are really doing is A) showing you have an interest in that individual, B) helping them relate to you better as a person, C) decreasing their level of fear when they talk to you, and D) um, something else I can't remember…"

"Helping them realize you're human too and you have some of the same fears and concerns they do?" Malik added.

"Yes! What Malik said," Andrea agreed. "So praise them if they deserve it, but otherwise, it can be anything, like, 'How are you feeling? Over that cold yet?' Or 'supposed to be great weather this weekend. Got any big plans?' Or 'how about those Maple Leafs?' Or maybe, 'Did you watch *Game of Thrones* last night?'"

"Oh! Oh, heck, you mean we can just chit chat?" Megan asked.

Reese nodded. "I get it now. It doesn't have to be any big deal, but you have enough of those interactions and they get more comfortable around you. Then when you do have to be negative, they're not afraid of you; they trust you more because you're like them. And, by the way, we don't live in Toronto, so 'how about those Maple Leafs' was a crummy suggestion."

Everyone laughed.

"Reese is too correct," Andrea pointed out. "It's good when you guys point out my mistakes. It means you're comfortable talking to me and that's how we really communicate. Humor is a great tool, and when the day comes that the employees start making jokes about you, to your face, that's the day you know you're a positive manager."

"Or that they really *do* think you're a joke," Reese suggested.

They all laughed again.

"I'm getting it. So when they are comfortable with you, then they should be more open to whatever it is we have to say, right?" Meghan asked.

"Now you've got it," Andrea said as she sipped her beer.

Meghan smiled broadly. "So I should create a spreadsheet and track positive versus negative conversations with every employee on my lines?"

"Absolutely not," Andrea said, shaking her head. "Keep it real. Tracking all that makes it phony. I'm just saying take advantage of every opportunity you get to chat with people about anything. You know, when you're talking with someone on the line, basically everybody within four feet of that person can hear too. So take advantage of that. Talk to all of them at once. Or just know they are listening. If my boss showed an interest in one of my coworkers and was laughing or having an upbeat conversation with him, I'd make a mental note to myself saying, 'He's not so bad. Seems like a nice guy—or woman,' as the case may be. Remember, you're trying to enhance their perception of you as a positive manager. Every step you take in that direction helps you when you have to do some serious coaching with someone."

"So don't try to count up the number of good interactions to make sure you do five to one or higher?" Malik asked.

"No. Just keep it in mind, and that's, well, that's the secret. Knowing it has to be far more positive interactions than you're probably having now, and doing it, will make every employee more responsive to you when you coach them," Andrea said.

The team discussed the concept and specific interactions for the next forty minutes as the evening wore on. Andrea reminded them that this was only one tactic and that with more time focused on educating the supervisors, they could all improve their business skills, and there was much more they could learn—a handy skill in any management position.

"Andrea, when we started this conversation, you said you wanted to educate the line workers, too. How would we do that?" Reese asked.

"Oh, boy, I did, didn't I?" Andrea admitted. "Well, that's a very important part of this process. I'm talking about educating them, in general, about business and about math so that they can help us solve some problems. But that is mostly something *I'll* have to do, and it's getting late, so I'll tell you about that some other day."

As they wrapped it up, Malik asked one more question. "Andrea, we started this out talking about things we can do to speed up our actions and get things done faster. I guess I'm not following how this positive to negative ratio deal speeds things up."

"It's a good question, Malik. Here's the short answer. If we can develop a positive relationship with all the employees, making change will come easier. They are less likely to fight us on every little thing if they trust us. We have to build that trust one individual relationship at a time. And when we do that, we can start moving faster as a company."

Guessing that her answer wasn't quite up to the task, she reached into her briefcase for the two pictures she had borrowed from her uncle. She placed them side by side.

"Who will win the race between these two boats?" Andrea paused for a moment, and knowing the answer was beyond obvious, she added, "When the employees trust us, they all get into the boat and row in the same direction. When that day comes, our competition will be left in our wake."

FRIDAY, MAY 11

At eight o'clock sharp, Reese gave a slight knock on Andrea's open door and got her attention.

"Got a minute?"

"You bet, come on in," Andrea replied.

As Reese sat down, he handed a sheet of paper to her and said, "These are the raises I have in mind this month. Wanted to make sure it was all OK with you."

Andrea gave the page a one-second look over and set it down. Looking directly at Reese, she said, "Remember a few meetings ago, we talked about the three questions you should ask yourself about each raise?"

"Um, yeah, I was here. I remember," Reese said.

"Is there anything unusual about these raises?"

Reese shook his head.

"Did you ask the three questions of yourself before deciding these are the raises you want to give?" Andrea asked.

"Yeah," Reese replied.

"Tell me what the three questions are," Andrea ordered.

"Andrea, you created them, why do I—oh, you want to know if *I* remember them?"

Andrea just stared back, a small smile starting to break out on her face.

"Well, I do. They make sense. Number one: Is the raise I intend to give in the normal range? Number two: If it isn't, can I defend it to Andrea and any other employee who hears about it and gets upset? Number three: Do I feel confident that what I'm doing is in the best interests of the company and the employee?"

"Very good," Andrea said. "Let me ask you, do you like micromanagers?"

"Uh, no. Nobody does."

"So why are we having this conversation?"

"Well, I…I just thought you'd want to see what I was doing before I did it."

"Well, in this case, you're wrong. I hired you because I believe in you and in your ability to make good decisions. I like having people like you and Meghan and Malik working with me because you need no micromanagement. If you already looked at all the raises you propose and answered *yes* to all three questions, then I totally trust your judgment. Go ahead and do it and just attach the raise summary sheet to your next weekly report to bring me up to date."

Reese stared back at Andrea for a moment, eyeing her to see if he missed something. Then a smile erupted on his face and he said, "I got it. Thanks!"

Before she could even reply, he had bolted from the chair and was halfway out her door.

Andrea chuckled to herself and returned to her paperwork.

At 11:15, Preston Mays entered Andrea's office, right on time for his appointment. She had called him two days ago to set it up and sent him the specs on the project she had in mind. After seeing his bid, she considered shopping it around some more, but remembering what Uncle Tyler had said about taking advantage of the green light, she accepted his offer yesterday.

Before Preston sat down, Andrea escorted him down the stairs to the floor and showed him the operation. She pointed out the white board they had placed high on the wall, and they watched as one of the workers climbed the ladder and updated the figures on the board.

"So, as you can see, we keep track of several numbers up there, including today's total, which is only at 78 so far, and the monthly total, which you see is…" Andrea stalled for a moment as the new total was being updated. When the worker finished writing, she finished, "At 1,902. So now you've seen the process we have today, and I don't know about you, but it reminds me of, you know, the 1950s."

Preston laughed. "Yes, it is a bit outdated."

"Just a tiny bit," Andrea agreed.

They returned to her office, and Preston described what he envisioned. "Based on what you wrote in your email, I see the need for a computer console at the beginning of Line 1 and the end of Line 6. The origin point would be where the operator entered the item type by the classification number and the dollar value of the item. At the end point, the operator would identify if the product was fully complete or if it was going to the reject pile. Both locations would be time stamped at the moment of entry and the program would automatically update the number of daily shipments, the number of monthly shipments, the percentage that figure represents of the pre-assigned goal, and the extrapolated finish number for the month at that moment in time. Does that sound right?"

"That would be wonderful. And it would get my workers off that scary ladder. That alone makes it worthwhile," Andrea said. Pausing for a moment, she followed up with another question. "What about the other statistics?"

"I'm happy to say we figured out how to do that, too. We'll program the display screen to switch to a new view for one minute out of every five. It will display the number of units and types that are currently on the belts for each line and the total number of each classification of unit for the day and month. Plus, as you requested, the classification number will be tied to the parts and supplies used and it will instantly update inventory totals. That will all be real time data."

"And the total dollar amount in the employee bonus pool plus the individual full-time share amount will show up too, right?" Andrea asked.

Preston hesitated. "It, um, certainly *can*. Technically there's no problem displaying any number you want, but I do have a concern about whether the dollar amount and all the other data you requested should be posted."

"There's a problem with it?" Andrea asked.

"Well, how should I say this? Um, it's usually not the kind of information our clients really want to have the employees see. Displaying the total revenue from the items for the day and month and the current labor cost as a percentage of that may, uh, you know, cause some employee unrest. I could get the program to create a 'management eyes only' report for you so you could certainly get that data."

Andrea just looked at him. "Mr. Mays, I want them to know. I am in the process of educating them about the realities of business, and I can do that best when I am trusted and when my credibility is strong. A high degree of transparency creates that kind of trust. I want them to get the feedback *and* to see the numbers. *All* the numbers."

Preston rubbed his chin. "It's unorthodox to say the least. What about the productivity numbers? The ones that show units per hour, revenue per hour, average units per line minute, and the others?"

"Yes," Andrea replied with an unwavering voice. "I want an educated workforce. We can't make ourselves better if we do things the same way we always have. I want to be immersed in the twenty-first century, and if Juggernaut doesn't do this, sooner or later a competitor will. And the one who adapts the fastest to this new world's pace of change will be the one who wins."

Deciding not to argue with a paying customer, Preston rose from his seat and said, "OK, sounds like you know what you're doing. I'll get my crew working on it, and honestly it's not that hard. I'll have a finished product for you within three weeks. Did you select a TV screen yet to connect to it?"

"I did. I'll be getting a 120-inch screen with a 16:9 ratio."

"That's all I needed to know. You, Ms. Lane, will have a state of the art information system providing dynamite feedback to you and your workers and we'll be able to make changes and add other stats to that as you go along. Should be ready by the end of the month."

They shook hands, and as Mr. Mays left her office, she allowed herself a satisfied smile. She hadn't bothered to ask permission to spend thousands on the project. She was taking full advantage of her green light and doing what she was sure was right. Getting quality real time data—automatically updating inventory, eliminating the need for personalized feedback reports every week, and using it to help educate the employees as well as management— was a giant step forward.

Bentley would never do this. He doesn't value real time data. He only chooses to save money, as if investing in the future were a foreign idea to him. The bankers will get it. They see this set up and we'll score some great points. I'm not slowing down again for anybody.

SATURDAY, MAY 12

Andrea took another bite of her blueberry muffin as her uncle tried to summarize what she had told him. "So, on Thursday, you met with Sammi, the HR person, and talked about working more closely together to hire better workers for the lines, right?" Not really waiting for her to confirm, he continued, "And she said that she was going to work on improving the whole meet-and-greet process and create a video about how you and the manufacturing crew do business."

Andrea nodded.

"And then last night, you met with Sales Manager Gretchen and she said she instituted the new bonus program you two designed and snagged herself a top-notch sales rep who now felt he could make some real money. And…uh, what was the other thing she's doing?"

Andrea put her coffee cup down and replied, "I told her about the new software and what we could track and she said she had been asking Bentley for two years to give her real time data on what items are selling, so inventory wouldn't run behind demand and she could see what was hot and was not."

"Oh, yeah. I like that one, by the way. So now she'll be able to get the same reports you do and her problem will be solved?"

Again Andrea nodded, smiling more broadly this time.

"Andi, you're doing great. Moving fast. Making decisions. And now you're going to start the employee education part. How are you going to tackle that?"

"I'm not sure. If only I knew someone with a business education background who could guide me," Andrea said, pretending to be lost in thought.

"Oh, that's a tough one," Tyler said, smirking.

He took a sip of his coffee, waiting for her to follow up. When she didn't, he blurted out, "Damn! I love this stuff. I'll have an outline for you by Monday."

"Yes! I was hoping you'd say that."

Tyler laughed. "We're having some fun now! I got it almost written in my head already. First of all, you paint the big picture about why you are doing this for them, then you have to start slow and small—pick one good example of a simple business math problem and walk them through it. Help them get their feet wet."

Tyler went on for another sixty minutes while Andrea took notes and marveled at her uncle's depth of knowledge. When they finished, she headed to the office and walked around the floor, waiting for the inspiration she knew would hit her. After a brief time, she knew what example she'd use to help the employees grasp a basic process of business.

Uncle Tyler's right. This is going to be fun!

TUESDAY, MAY 15

After announcing on Monday that she would hold the first optional Juggernaut business training class for the manufacturing workers on this coming Wednesday night, and trying hard to overcome the quizzical looks on all their faces, she realized a big part of the battle would be getting people to attend.

On Tuesday, adopting the wise counsel of her supervisors, she announced that the local sub shop was catering the evening and those who wanted to stay after work for an hour would have salads and a variety of sandwiches to select from. Within minutes, the number of employees signing up rose from six to seventeen.

As everyone finished their day, Andrea hung out by the time clock and urged more to attend. By the end of the Tuesday shift, the number rose to nineteen.

Satisfied that she would have a reasonable turnout, Andrea headed back to her office to finish her PowerPoint presentation for the meeting. Before she reached the top of the stairs to her level, she heard a familiar voice calling to her.

"Andrea, wait up," Robbie yelled out.

She turned and saw Robbie and Gretchen heading toward the stairs at a rapid clip.

"What's up?" Andrea asked as they moved closer.

"That's our question for you, girl," Gretchen replied. "Everybody's talking about this educational class you're holding tomorrow. We want to know what you're doing this time."

They all entered her office together, and Robbie wasted no time at all. "So you didn't think to tell us about your secret meeting?"

Andrea shook her head. "Sorry, it's not secret. I've been so busy I forgot to tell you guys. I just believe that a more educated workforce will help us to move faster and make more productive changes. So I want to start in on it right away before…you know, before Bentley tells me not to do it."

Gretchen still wore a puzzled expression on her face. "I guess I still don't really understand. What are you going to talk about?"

Andrea patted her laptop and said, "I've been working on it here. Dale is going to connect my laptop so I can show the view on the big screen. Mostly, I'm just talking about our business and helping them understand why we're creating change and how the math works and, well, kind of the big picture of it all."

"It's never a bad thing to educate the crew more, but how does that help speed up the changes we need to make?" Robbie asked.

"I, um, I had a long talk with my uncle and he keeps urging me to get the workers more involved. He says when they really get it, they'll start giving us a whole slew of ideas on how we can do better. When it's their own idea, they already have buy-in. All I have to do is give them credit, and after a while, I believe they'll start making change themselves. When we can get to the point where they're embracing change instead of fighting it, then we'll be on a roll and we'll start eating the competition's lunch instead of the other way around."

Robbie and Gretchen stared back at her. Their wheels turning, she gave them a minute to comment.

Finally, Robbie said, "So is this a manufacturing event only?"

He could tell Andrea wasn't understanding the question, so he elaborated, "I mean, I bet some of my guys would like to attend tomorrow night."

"I think I oughta make it mandatory for the sales reps to be there, too," Gretchen added.

Smiling broadly now, Andrea replied, "The more the merrier. We should let Sammi know too."

"Cool. Better order some more sandwiches," Robbie said, smiling.

WEDNESDAY, MAY 16

A t 5:15, using the cordless mic, Andrea urged everyone to find a seat and quiet down. She looked out at the crowd and was glad she had nearly doubled the food order.

"OK, one hour tonight and then we'll have ourselves some eats," Andrea said.

Over thirty people were there, and every one of them stared back at her. Dale flicked a few switches and the lights dimmed to 40 percent as the large screen on the wall showed the Welcome page.

Hoping that she had prepared well enough, Andrea began, "First, I want to thank so many of you for coming and giving this a chance. Over thirty of you is a super start for us. I'd like to think you're here to enjoy my fantastic presentation, but I know it's really for the food, right?"

Everyone laughed, and one of the men in the back called out, "Yeah, and speaking of food, where is it?"

Again a round of laughter as Andrea pointed to the employee and said, "There's always a comedian around. It's on its way. Should arrive at six, and we'll wrap up at 6:15 so you can all stuff your faces. Deal?"

Andrea got a generally happy nod from most of the audience, and she thought to herself, *OK, Uncle Tyler. Step one, get 'em to laugh and loosen up. Check.*

"All right, take a look at the screen. Our first order of business is to discuss why we are here tonight."

"For the food!" the comedian yelled out.

Andrea chuckled and continued, "Right, but beyond that, why are we spending time and money to do this? I'll tell you. This world is not standing still for anyone. The pace of change is speeding up, and five or ten years from now, no business will really be the same. In order for us to stay relevant, build our customer base, and continue to create jobs, we have to be one step ahead of the pace of change. Or at least staying even with it. And how do you imagine we can do that?"

She paused to see if anyone wanted to volunteer anything. Barely able to wrap their heads around the problem, no one ventured any ideas.

Andrea looked to the VP of Logistics. "Robbie, you have an opinion on that?"

"I think," Robbie started. He hesitated, then continued, "I think having a more educated workforce—a workforce that understands their industry better and is closer to the real work than upper management—is a healthy thing. And the better they understand it all, the easier it will be to adapt and dream up new solutions that we haven't had before."

Andrea flashed him a grateful smile. "Couldn't have said it better myself. So, like Robbie said, we don't really know what challenges or opportunities are going to come our way in this business in the future, but I think it makes sense to educate everyone as much as we can in preparation for having to move fast. In this new world now, where cell phones are practically obsolete before they are out of the box and where consumers repair nothing and replace everything without giving it a second thought, we need to improve on so many levels to give them what they want and to protect our jobs. And we have to grow more nimble to be able to shift gears and go in new directions."

She paused for brief moment to let that sink in, then said, "So what I believe—"

"Wait a minute!" Ricky yelled out. "Is this just some big build-up to announcing job cuts? You said we have to protect our jobs."

"We do, Ricky. But I have no other agenda tonight other than to begin a process of education for everyone. Right now, I'm thinking we may need more people, not fewer. I had a meeting just a few days ago with Sammi about lining up some new hires before we need them."

"Yeah, management protecting each other's butts. I'm not really believin' you."

"I understand. You didn't believe me when we changed the pay raise policy, and you didn't believe me when I said the bonus program could pay you more than the old base pay. All I can do is keep trying to show you that what you see is what you get with me. I get why you're concerned."

Ricky stood up and pointed his finger at Andrea. "So you guarantee there won't be any layoffs?"

"Ricky, you got kids, right?" Andrea asked.

"Yeah, two boys."

Andrea nodded. "If they asked you if you could guarantee that nothing bad would ever happen to them, what would you say?"

Ricky's face turned red and he stuttered his reply. "I-I'd tell 'em, as, uh, as long as I was around, nothing bad would ever happen to 'em."

Andrea stared back at him for a moment and said, "You're a good dad, Ricky. Sometimes we have to say that. But I don't want to talk down to you like you're little kids. You're all adults. You deserve the truth, so that's what I'm telling ya. There are no plans right now contemplating layoffs. Sales are getting stronger, and our goal is to fine tune procedures so that we are more productive and ready for growth. But this world is a volatile place, and no one in their right business mind can promise anything or give any guarantees. That's one reason we're doing this. I don't want anyone here to feel like a helpless victim. If everyone is educated more, then you all have a better chance to be the masters of your own fate. So, anyone else with concerns they want to talk about?"

Ricky sat back down, and a more somber crowd than before sat quietly. No one spoke up.

Andrea checked her notes and mentally checked off another of Uncle Tyler's milestones: *Tell them why they're here. Check.*

Andrea moved forward. On the screen was a picture of a large Glimmer Stone Value Vase, Juggernaut's signature sales item.

"I struggled over this part for tonight's meeting," Andrea began. "I want to do *one* thing tonight that helps you understand the finances better, but I don't want to bore you out of your minds. Let me see, raise your hand if math was your favorite subject in school."

She looked around. An accountant from Tim's department and two other men on the lines raised their hands. One woman raised hers but tentatively pulled it back.

Spotting her, Andrea pointed her way and called out, "Is that Debbie? Not sure?"

"I like math," Debbie answered back. "But I think I liked history better."

Many around her nodded their agreement.

"OK, so we have three of you that liked math. A little less than ten percent. So I'm going to keep this simple, and I believe it will enlighten every one of you. We're going to look at how much every large Glimmer Stone vase costs to sell, produce, package, ship, and get into the customers' hands."

For the next thirty minutes, Andrea left the picture of the vase on the screen. One by one, she discussed the individual costs of creating the final product. As she did, she moved to the next slide and the vase changed color from the base, working its way toward the top. Each extra layer of color represented another expense.

She showed them the vase shell first and explained how it represented the cost of buying vase shells in bulk and storing them. Then she showed the cost of the Glimmer Stones, drawing many a shocked expression. She continued with the average cost of labor on the lines, then the packaging and shipping, the sales commissions, the cost of advertising, the share of overhead, the prorated office staff costs, and generally ticked down the entire list, showing what the total cost burden was for one vase.

When she finished, the cost covered the very top of the large vase and it totaled $434. She stared back at the crowd as the catering crew entered and began setting up the food for everyone.

"Our timing is pretty good. It's ten after six, and I bet just a few of you are hungry. Next Wednesday, we're going to talk about how we decide what to charge for these vases, and I'd love it if each of you would think about how you think we should come up with that number. Especially because it's one of the most important decisions the company makes.

"Before we break, does anyone have any questions?"

She looked around as no one raised a hand or stood up. Finally, Sue Anderson stood and said, "Andrea, most companies like to keep it a mystery. They don't tell what things really cost. So, um, well, why are you telling us this?"

Andrea looked back at Sue and replied, "You said it yourself, most companies don't ever have this conversation. So, my answer to you is that's why they fail. The last thing we want to be like is 'most companies.'"

Seeing no more questions, Andrea dismissed them. "Those sandwiches and salads look mighty lonely over there. You guys are good at solving problems; let's solve that one, too."

The chairs were emptied in no time. As everyone had their fill of food and drinks, Andrea found herself surrounded by employees, each with a boatload of questions they couldn't wait to unleash on her.

SATURDAY, MAY 19

Robbie turned down Delano Street and found a parking spot right in front of the bar. He looked at his passenger and quipped, "Look at that! Five feet from the entrance. Pretty good, huh?"

Andrea shook her head and said, "Don't get all full of yourself. It's Saturday morning. There's lots of parking spots open."

"Always raining on my parade. You sure your uncle doesn't mind that I'm tagging along for a free breakfast?"

"I'm sure. He suggested it," Andrea said.

"Why? I mean, why me?"

"'Cuz he knows we've gone out a few times and he wants to size you up. And he wants to hear some of your brilliant business ideas."

"Oh, yeah, I'll bet," Robbie said. "Like the high school dropout is going to teach a university Economics Professor a thing or two."

Andrea shot him a glance.

"Long story," Robbie admitted, wishing he hadn't said that. "I returned and finished. I'll tell you about it someday."

Andrea pushed the door open and they entered. After introductions were done, the requisite small talk wrapped up as Tyler's ham-and-eggs breakfast was being served.

Robbie waited for Andrea to take a bite first, then he shoveled in his first mouthful. "Mmmm, that's good. So the university professor can cook, too, huh?"

"I've had some practice," Tyler said. Looking Robbie's way, he continued, "Now, the way this works is I con Andrea into telling me about her whole week while I quietly eat. She's very accommodating. Feel free to join me."

Andrea rolled her eyes and began filling her uncle in on the events of the past few days. As she finished, she let out a long breath and attacked her plate a bit more aggressively.

Tyler pondered all she'd said and summarized, "So, overall, you think it went well, even though, um, Dicky asked some tough—"

"Ricky, not Dicky," Andrea corrected.

"Whatever," Tyler said. "He's the troublemaker. Stan didn't show up, right?"

"He said he had another appointment," Andrea replied.

"Maybe. Maybe not. Maybe he just didn't want to get caught in the crossfire between you and Ricky. But, either way, it sounds like you handled it well."

"She did," Robbie interjected. "I mean, you can't win an argument like that. She let him say his piece and she calmly answered. She was a lot more composed than I would have been."

"I believe it," Tyler said. "I've watched her grow up a lot in the last few months. She's become quite the student of human nature."

"I think you have to be these days," Robbie said. "I mean, so much of running a business or department now is all about people management. If you can't communicate effectively, you're already screwed."

"Too true. She's getting better at working the crowd, too. Get 'em loose, crack a few jokes, make them feel comfortable, then hit the serious topics," Tyler added.

"She did all that, and then she brought the food in and the best part was everybody wanted to hang out and talk some more. On their own time," Robbie said, shaking his head in wonder.

Tyler looked at his niece and asked, "You have anything more to add to that?"

"Yeah. It was fun listening to you two guys go on and on about how well I did. What chatterboxes you are. And for a change, I got to eat while you talked."

"OK, just for that, no dessert for you," Tyler said.

"I'm devastated," Andrea joked. "Especially since we never have a dessert with our breakfast, but I'll have some more coffee if you're pouring."

Tyler got up from the table to retrieve the coffee pot. As he did, he asked, "How are they doing on the computer program to display all that data on the big screen?"

Andrea swallowed the last of her eggs and said, "You won't believe it! They think they are done already. More than a week early. They want to install it on Friday."

Tyler filled their cups and said, "That's great. I don't think you can underestimate the impact of this. Not only do you get real time data, but the workers also get instant reinforcement. So many companies overlook the importance of the rank and file getting reinforcement, too. I bet they're gonna love it."

Andrea, less certain of that, replied, "I hope so. I'm doing it mostly for the bankers, so they can see some real change in the manufacturing process."

"Andi," Tyler said, as he eyed her suspiciously. "Did you order this scoreboard to increase the momentum?"

"Uh…I'm sorry—what's the question?"

"Did you order the making of the scoreboard to jack up the momentum?"

"Well, I heard ya, but I don't even understand the question," Andrea replied.

"OK, OK, sorry. Maybe you did it instinctively," Tyler suggested.

"Unc? Did what?"

"Look, it's a…a change strategy. When you are in the middle of a long project and people are losing interest or just sort of getting bored, that's when many major change programs falter and die.

So the strategy is to do something, practically anything, that gives everyone a boost. You know, shake things up a bit. And nothing is more effective than a physical change to the work environment. Laying out the lines differently, adding new furniture, painting the building—something that gets their attention and reminds them of all the changes that they are making happen. It's a momentum booster. Your scoreboard is doing that for you."

Andrea glanced at Robbie and then back to her uncle. Smiling, she said, "Um, yeah, that's what I was doing, all right. What you said."

"Nice bluff, but I don't think he's buying it," Robbie added, laughing.

Tyler laughed too and said, "Very good, Andrea. Next time say it with a little more conviction and someone might buy it. Of course, it may have been sort of instinctual, which I guess is even better. In any case, I like the idea of the scoreboard a lot."

Robbie nodded and added, "Andi, I think you're missing something else here."

"What?" she asked.

"Well, Tyler can correct me here if he thinks I'm wrong, but almost eighty percent of your workforce on the lines is male. Guys' DNA is kinda hardwired to be competitive. I think most of the line workers will be staring at the numbers on the screen to see how they're doing. I think it's gonna spur on more productivity."

Andrea stared at Robbie, then turned to Tyler. "Does that sound right to you, Unc?"

"He may have a damn good point, Andi. Guys relate to goals and records in numerical format pretty strongly. Certainly many women do, too, but I can see them watching the numbers and trying to top their previous bests. I think he's right."

"It's not a competition, guys. I mean, we're not pitting one line against the other. There's no bragging rights here."

Tyler shook his head. "I disagree. Look at baseball players. They all have personal and team goals at the beginning of the season. Every time they come to the plate, they see the scoreboard and it shows them hitting .276 or whatever. If a player's goal is, say,

.280 or higher, then he finds incentive in that. They want the next hit just a bit more. You are giving these workers a scoreboard of their own. Reinforcement, especially immediate reinforcement, is a powerful motivator and it needs to be built right into your process. You're doing that, and it will pay off."

Andrea chuckled. "Guy talk. Are you sure you don't want to be alone so you can have a meaningful conversation, like who was better, Oscar Robertson or Kobe Bryant?"

"Ooh," Robbie said quietly. "Attacking sports. Not a friendly thing to say to two guys trying to help."

"Not friendly at all," Tyler agreed, suppressing his smile.

"OK," Andrea said, caving in just a bit. "I'll believe it. But don't go trying to convince me that the DNA makes men better workers than women. I mean, then you'd have to know something about women, too."

"We do!" both Robbie and Tyler said at the same time. Then they fist bumped to celebrate.

"Oh, guys can be so juvenile sometimes. I think I'm going to be ill. Robbie, you better take me home quick," Andrea said, then chuckled her way to the door.

Tyler laughed too but then got more serious. "Andi, seriously, keep this up. Don't let up. Full court press all the way to the finish line, OK?"

"You're mixing your sports analogies. But I got it. I'll keep the pressure on," she called back over her shoulder.

As they left the bar, Tyler watched and mumbled to himself, "Atta girl. Full court press. Andrea *Express* Lane."

WEDNESDAY, MAY 23

Gathered on the manufacturing floor again, nearly forty workers and Andrea were ten minutes into the second BizEd meeting. Andrea had just finished summarizing what had been discussed on the 16th for everyone and now was moving on to the pricing issues.

"So, as a reminder, we identified all the components of costs of a typical large Glimmer Stone Vase and that came to $434. So the next question is, what should we price it at?"

She looked out over the crowd and waited for someone to raise their hand.

After a few moments, a man who works on Line 3 raised his hand.

Recognizing him from the time she spent on that line, Andrea pointed to him and said, "Phil, what do you think?"

Phil scrunched his face up and shook his head. "Look, Andrea, I don't want to sound like an idiot, but, I mean, I spent too much college time in philosophy and not enough—well hell, not any time in business classes. But it seems we already identified the cost. Why can't we just sell it for that? It pays for everything and, you know, maybe we could market ourselves as the company that's not obsessed with profits."

Andrea acknowledged that concept and said, "I like your marketing angle, Phil, but there are some pretty good reasons for needing to make a profit on every item. So, for example—"

"Here it comes!" Ricky called out. "Profit first, people second or third or fourth."

Andrea stopped talking and looked Ricky's way. "OK, good, we have a skeptic in our group. It's always a good thing to question our actions to reanalyze if they are the smart thing to do or not. Who has any ideas about why we should aim for a profit on every sale?"

A hand in the back was raised, and Andrea immediately recognized it was from one of the accounting assistants in the CFO's office.

She nodded to him, and he stood and said, "Uh, I'm Doug in Accounting. One of the costs you missed on the vase was credit card fees. We pay three point two percent right now, so on the current price of a large Value Vase, that's an additional…uh…nineteen dollars or so. Since about a third of our sales are by credit card, gotta figure in an additional six or seven dollars at least."

"You're right, Doug, we did miss that. Can you think of any other—"

Anticipating her question, Doug added, "Well, yeah. You gotta allow for contingencies. You know, surprise expenses. We don't budget for them, but they happen. Like the repairs we needed to do to the backup generator after the blackout."

"Another excellent point, Doug, thank you. Anyone else?"

A woman form Line 4 called out, "Our benefits get more expensive every year. Don't we have to account for that?"

Again Andrea nodded and said, "Yes, we do. Everything changes constantly. Vendors raise their rates, banks change their terms, taxes go up. It's almost impossible to plan for everything, so you either have to add some mystery amount to the costs or you have to make some kind of profit that covers it.

"There are other things, too. You folks all made more money from bonuses for the last few months. A lot of that was a result of being more productive. When you get more product made, the company makes more money, so we share that with you via the bonuses. If we broke even on every item, then all the increased productivity in the world wouldn't create extra cash. Plus, where would your raises come from if we didn't make profit? You get raises because in one way or another we see you as someone who is adding value and helping us be more productive."

Andrea paused to judge whether or not she was reaching people. "Any other ideas?"

A sales rep raised his hand and asked, "Did you already count the commissions to the sales reps?"

Andrea nodded. "Yes, we did."

"Well, what about the discounts we give to the big bulk buyers for early payment or just volume discounts?"

Andrea glanced at Gretchen and said, "Funny you should mention that. Gretchen, our Marketing VP, is going to talk all about marketing at our next meeting, and she will delve into that issue, too. But you're right, we didn't include discounts in the formula."

Sensing there were no more suggestions, Andrea moved on to a major point that she wanted to make. "There is one other very important issue concerning why we need to price our items correctly for a reasonable profit. That is the banks. See, every six months or so, our bank loans us about six million dollars to replenish inventory and cover payroll. Then we pay that back over the next six months with interest. The interest is about five percent, so that's almost $50,000 in interest costs every month. Not only did we not include that yet in our cost analysis, but here's the kicker."

She paused for effect. "See, the bank has all this money from the depositors that they *want* to lend out to qualified borrowers. There are never enough qualified borrowers because the bank managers want to be able to sleep at night. They aren't in the *risk* business. They don't want to take any chances, so they only loan to companies that can convince them that they are making enough profit to pay back the loan. For our industry, if we aren't making a minimum of twenty percent profit on a regular basis, they won't even talk to us. And if they don't loan us the money, well, we're out of business. So, I see the food is being delivered now, and everybody's getting hungry, so let's take fifteen more minutes and then wrap this up. I'm hoping everyone understands better why we have to make a reasonable profit. Here's my question to you. In light of all we just discussed, I'd say the cost of each large vase is probably closer to $450."

Again she paused. "So how much should we sell them for?"

A dozen hands shot up. Andrea looked around, happy to see how many had opinions. "Just shout your numbers out," she ordered.

The room was filled with a cacophony of voices calling out numbers anywhere between $460 and $900. Andrea encouraged more responses, and when nearly everyone had voiced their opinion, she said, "Excellent! I've heard a lot of good ideas out there. Keep those thoughts, and we'll pick this conversation back up at our next meeting."

"You're not going to tell us what the right answer is?" one of the line workers asked.

"I'll tell you this—something most of you probably know already—currently the vase sells for $589. And here is one of most exciting aspects of business—we don't *know* the correct answer. Five eighty-nine is our best guess. That is the question we'll tackle at the next meeting, and we can't wait to hear your thoughts on that."

She spotted a few surprised faces and arched her eyebrows at them playfully. "OK, let's eat!"

THURSDAY, MAY 24

In a dark corner booth at Brannigan's, a server dropped off two drinks for the patrons. Tim raised his glass to Craig and got an uninspired half-effort response from his friend.

"That damn woman. She's telling them everything," Craig said.

"I heard she was discussing profit margin last night. Can you believe that?"

Craig fixed an angry stare at Tim and said, "Yeah, and you know who helped? Your two assistants, for crying out loud. They volunteered extra information—specifics on some of our costs. Nice coaching, Tim," he said, acerbity dripping from each syllable.

"Wait a minute! I didn't coach them. I didn't even know they were going to attend," Tim countered.

"No shit! You should have known, and you should've told them to keep their mouths shut," Craig fired back.

They sipped at their drinks in an uneasy silence for several minutes. Finally, Tim asked, "So what are we going to do now?"

"She's becoming more influential and popular, so Plan C, I guess."

"We've got a Plan C?" Tim asked.

"I got a Plan D, too, but it sucks. Look, all we can do now is prepare our plan to make the numbers look as bad as we can after we get the loan and I'll keep schmoozing the bank. When our meeting in July comes, we'll convince Bentley to take a lucrative retirement package, I'll claim credit for most of what little Miss Sunshine has been doing, and the banks will give us the money we need and give me control. You and I will pay off Bentley for a while, then find a way to ease Lane out and tell the boss how terrible things are and cut his retirement money so far down he'll agree to sell to us. It'll delay our ownership, but once we get it, we'll suck this baby dry, default on the last loan, and exit stage left, leaving the bank and the employees holding the bag."

Tim smiled. "I like it. I can handle a short delay for a guaranteed sweet retirement."

"Me too," Craig said. "Let's get one more drink for the road."

WEDNESDAY, MAY 30

At four o'clock, Andrea was summoned to Mr. Bentley's office. She showed up a minute early and was shown in.

Bentley wasted no time. "I hear you're doing another one of those employee education meetings tonight."

Andrea swallowed hard and replied, "Yes, sir. It starts at 5:15."

"I thought it was a just a passing fancy, but you do one every week. I don't want you to do any more."

"Sir, what we are doing will benefit the company in the long run. Explaining the—"

"Cancel it. I said no more," Bentley barked.

Taking a moment to collect herself, she continued, "Explaining the math of the problems we face makes the workers realize how linked they all are to the company's success or failure. That's a positive thing. It's part of what makes change more possible here."

"I heard you were going to talk about marketing and pricing. I don't like that."

"Mr. Bentley, with all due respect, the world is changing now so fast, we have to do everything we can to keep up with it. A competitor could come up with a product tomorrow that could devastate one or more of our product lines. We have to be ready. We have to be one step ahead of them."

"We've done just fine for fifty years. No one has found a way to beat us yet," Bentley said.

"That just makes us ripe for the plucking. *You* told us we had to change things and produce more. That's what I'm trying to do."

"I know, and now I'm saying enough. I've had enough change. Cancel the meeting."

Andrea sighed. "It would be a waste of a lot of food. Why don't you come down and join us? It would mean a lot to the employees."

"Damn it! Don't you ever do anything you're told!" Bentley screamed.

"Sir, I'm doing exactly as I was told. Exactly as you told us all back in January. And because I am following your directions, the bank is going to like what we're doing and make the loan to us."

She didn't wait for his reply. She left his office and returned to her own. It was forty seconds and two hallways later before she realized she'd been holding her breath since she walked away from him.

At 5:15 precisely, the third BizEd meeting began. As usual, Andrea made a few jokes to loosen the crowd up, summarized the two previous meetings quickly, and turned the meeting over to Gretchen.

Being a natural at sales, Gretchen had no problem speaking to the crowd that had grown to fifty-three employees. She launched into her presentation where she discussed all the factors that go into every pricing decision: profit margin, local economy, cost of living, advertising plan, marketing strategy, the competition's products, Juggernaut's product quality, and many more.

As she gave a cursory explanation to each of those, she involved the audience, getting them to respond to her questions.

Feeling that Gretchen had the meeting well in hand, Andrea's eyes roved the room and she found that she couldn't spot Ricky. She slid over toward Reese and asked, "You seen Ricky around?"

Reese took on a wry grin. "I swapped one of my Line 3 workers to Malik for one of his on Line 2. I had a little chat with Ricky about improving, then I kept chatting with him every day—trying hard, by the way—to be positive most of the time. Yesterday, I had to coach him about moving the items along a little faster."

"He was holding the line up?" Andrea asked.

"He was. So I told him he wouldn't be seeing a raise until he resolved that issue."

"And?" Andrea asked, letting the word just hang there.

"He told me I had a bad attitude and described in copious detail where I could shove it. Then he threw his ID tag at me and said he quit."

Andrea didn't react. She was surprised at herself for not feeling like she wanted to cheer. Instead, she felt a sadness. "What we're doing isn't for everybody. It certainly rewards those who hustle more, but it shines a glaring spotlight on those who slack off."

"I thought you'd be happy," Reese said.

"So did I. But we did this to him, and frankly, this was probably the very best job someone like Ricky could ever have. Now it's gone."

"I don't think…" Reese paused as he struggled to find the right words. "I don't think he liked what he saw and heard at the first two meetings. He thought management was the enemy, and I think even he came around to understanding that sometimes they are and sometimes they're not. The real enemy is math."

"Yup, the irrefutable, undeniable power of numbers is really what we're up against. I hope he finds something good elsewhere, but, I don't know, that sounds like a longshot to me."

Gretchen glanced at the clock and saw its red digital figures displaying 6:00. She started to wrap it up. "So, remember, when you take all those things into account, you can come up with a quality price to set, but tomorrow is another day, and it may be time to change that price already. Such are the vagaries of marketing."

When she finished, she received a strong round of applause, and Andrea came back on stage.

"Now you know why I had Gretchen talk about marketing—she's forgotten more about sales than I'll ever know. Thank you, Gretchen!'

Another smattering of applause ensued, and Gretchen gave a cute bow.

"Next week I've asked Sammi to come up and tell you about our new procedures for attracting, interviewing, hiring, and training new recruits. She's upgraded it dramatically because as we add more people and/or more shifts, our goal is to get the very best."

"Not guys like Malik, right?" a male voice from the crowd yelled out.

Everybody laughed. "Oh, God, no," Andrea replied. "Not anyone that bad ever again. Don't worry, though, we used our secret strategy and promoted Malik to supervisor because he was so bad on the line."

Again everyone laughed, and Malik scratched his head and pretended to not understand, which resulted in more laughter.

"All right," Andrea began, "almost time for a fine feast again. You know our crowd gets bigger every time. I think we may be single-handedly turning the sub shop into a money-printing machine. Every time I turn around we're doubling the previous week's order.

"I got one more thought to wrap this up with. Concerning your thoughts on the price, let me—um, just a minute, looks like we have a special guest. Mr. Bentley is coming over to join us. How about a big round of applause for the man who is smart enough to value an educated workforce and considerate enough to make sure we don't go home hungry after these long Wednesdays!"

Everyone in the group turned around and gave a stirring round of applause to the company owner. Bentley froze in his tracks and stared back at them, and then, his façade cracking a bit, he smiled and waved. For just a second, Andrea thought he may have been enjoying the moment.

Seeing her chance, she pushed the envelope of truthfulness even farther. "Mr Bentley knows the value of a properly rewarded and appreciated work force and he personally authorized your new bonus program and all the changes we've made. We met today to talk, and he told me he believed you were the finest workforce in the industry."

Again another huge round of cheers went up.

Feeling a little bad about manipulating the workers so much, Andrea got back on topic and said, "I want to close out this meeting by reiterating a point that Gretchen made earlier. We don't know for sure what the price point is. It may be higher than the $589 we are at now or it could be lower.

"But one thing we do know for sure is that this world is changing very fast and we have to be up to the task of changing along with it.

"Gretchen talked about new competition that is well-healed financially coming into our market and trying to steal market share. This kind of thing happens all the time. Someone may come in with a cheaper way to make Glimmer Stone Vases. They could undercut us by two hundred dollars and steal so much of our business that we'd have to close. They wouldn't care that they lost some money on every sale because after we were gone, they could raise their prices up and be the only player in the industry.

"Now I'm not trying to paint an ugly picture here just before you eat, but think about it. That could happen, and you'd ask, 'What can we do?' And I'm here to tell you, we are already doing it. We are becoming a production-oriented team. We're becoming a nimble force that isn't afraid of change. We're becoming the industry leader, and it's due to one thing and one thing only—you're smarter and you've embraced change rather than fighting it. In this world, the company that can do that can't be beat. Mr. Bentley, Sammi, Gretchen, Robbie, all your supervisors, and I are so damn proud of you."

Andrea stopped talking and started clapping. "Let's eat!"

The employees stood up and gave themselves a round of applause as well, then made a beeline to the food.

Robbie slid over next to Andrea and whispered, "Nice speech. Glad to hear you finally say something that was true."

Andrea turned to him, eyes wide and eyebrows arched. "What do you mean?"

"I mean that stuff about Bentley, well, let's just say if there was even a grain of truth to that, it would have been hard to see with the world's largest telescope."

Andrea chuckled. "It was, um, strategic. Yeah, that's the word—strategic. That's my story and I'm sticking to it."

Robbie pointed to the food line. Bentley was there filling up a plate alongside the line workers, smiling and laughing.

"Andi, I think maybe he likes the idea of being liked for a change. Did you plan that?"

Andrea shook her head. "No, but I saw the opportunity and I just took it. Full court press, remember?"

TUESDAY, JUNE 5

The May goal of four thousand was exceeded by twenty-three units, and June got off to a fabulous start. Having the new scoreboard in place and displaying up-to-date numbers was a big hit. Thomas still bellowed out the total whenever it hit an important number and everyone loved it.

Tonight, Andrea had a meeting scheduled at Brannigan's with Robbie, Gretchen, and Sammi, and she decided it was time to reach out to the other VPs again.

She stopped by the CFO's office and invited Tim to attend. He seemed surprised and unsure of how to respond.

"I, uh, I'll see if I have room in my schedule. What's the occasion?"

A bit wide-eyed, Andrea replied, "What's the occasion? How about we have exactly one month before the bank's doomsday? I think that qualifies as a good occasion."

Nearly speechless, Tim nodded his head and mumbled, "Well, we'll see."

She continued down the hall to Craig's office. His door was closed, and his secretary looked like she was about to tackle Andrea before she could just walk in.

"Can I help you, Ms. Lane?"

"Is Craig available? I only need two minutes."

Not bothering to answer, she pushed the intercom button and said, "Mr. Saunders, Ms. Lane is here to see you. She says it will only take two minutes."

Snapping back at her, he said, "Just a minute." Fifteen seconds later, his voice boomed out saying, "All right, send her in."

Ready for just about anything, Andrea opened his door and stepped into the room. "Craig," she said, giving him a one-syllable greeting.

"Andrea. What's up?"

"I thought you might want to join us for a drink at Brannigan's at five thirty. We've only got one month left before the bank meeting, and the other VPs and I are getting together to discuss what else we can do in the next thirty days."

Craig looked at her with accusing eyes. "So you think *you* should be the one to set up meetings now? I'm the leader here. I set the meetings up."

Andrea pursed her lips and said, "Well, don't you think we should have had a couple dozen of them already? I figure if you're not going to do it, I will."

"Damn presumptuous of you," Craig shot back.

"Hell, Craig, we'd be happy to attend if you cared enough to schedule one. We've had our own meetings before and neither you nor Tim has attended any since the first one at the start of the year. I thought you might want to hear what we're working on between now and July fifth."

"Well, you should've given me more notice. I'm busy tonight. Anything else?"

Andrea looked back at him and shook her head. "I guess not," she mumbled under her breath.

Being Tuesday, the crowd at Brannigan's was small and the gang of four had no problem claiming their favorite round-table booth. Andrea ordered some appetizers so they wouldn't be drinking on an empty stomach and started right in.

"You guys should know I invited Tim and Craig to attend. Craig said he was busy and Tim didn't appear to have much interest either."

Robbie rolled his eyes and said, "Yeah, boy, it's always a boring meeting when we're discussing how to save our jobs and those of all our employees. Too bad it wasn't something important."

Sammi smiled and put her nose up in the air and sniffed around. "I don't know about you folks, but I think I can smell a little sarcasm around here."

Gretchen jumped in. "I smell it too, Sammi. It's a special kind. It's justified-spot-on sarcasm. That kind is OK."

"Wait a minute," Robbie said. "I spoke too soon. Tim just walked in."

"Good," Andrea said. "Flag him down."

Robbie got his attention, and Tim came over and joined them.

"Sorry I'm late. Still got room for me?" Tim said, smiling like they were all his best friends.

They each moved over a bit and Tim scooted in.

"Tim, we were just going to go around the table and let everyone talk about their June initiative—you know, one last project to make happen before the meeting with the bank."

Tim nodded and looked around the table. A slight twitch of his lips caught their eyes.

Gretchen went first. She explained how she was putting several new policies in place to create a Rapid Response Team whose main function was to instantly give extra attention and care to any modest error or delay in getting the product to the customer. When she finished, she summed it up, saying, "So we think we can get a lot of mileage out of owning our mistakes right away and showing the customer that we care and are all about making it better. I think the positive PR from that far outweighs the cost. We'll be doing that starting June 15th."

Everyone complimented her on the strategy and added a few thoughts as to how their department can interact with that as well.

Before Andrea could move the conversation to the HR Department, Gretchen added, "And I'm also working with Andrea to form several new committees of hourly workers to monitor changes in competitor pricing or product lines. It'd be good to stay ahead of the bad guys for a change."

Andrea added a few comments about the value of employee participation on special projects like that, then turned to the next VP. "Sammi, what have you got?"

Sammi launched into the changes she was making in the HR Department, explaining how they are working with Andrea's three supervisors to make short videos about their jobs so that recruits can see what it's like. She also suggested that they select a day each week to pipe in some music to the manufacturing floor and the warehouse to raise spirits and break the monotony.

At the end, she added, "Here's the cool part. We were just filming some basic stuff on Line 2 yesterday and we hit unit number five hundred for the month. Thomas intoned it with his deep voice and the floor went crazy cheering and laughing. The camera man was sharp enough to move the view up to the new scoreboard where *500* was blinking on and off. I mean, it was exciting, and I think any recruit looking at that would think, you know, that this was a fun place to work. And it was just an accident that it happened."

"That is so cool, Sammi! Great work!" Andrea cooed. "We should do more of that—maybe some kind of training video explaining the bonus programs and start filming a minute before they hit one of the target levels so we get that cheering in the video, too."

Suddenly, Gretchen and Robbie both chimed in with ideas that impacted their department. Tim watched the dynamics of the group as his mouth hung open just a little too far.

Robbie told everyone about the latest changes in warehouse procedure and how he now had created four slightly different shifts, putting those employees who wanted different hours anyway into each one. Morale had boomed, and Andrea immediately insisted that Robbie meet with her supervisors to discuss the possibilities of doing similar tweaking to the manufacturing schedules.

When Robbie was finished, Andrea ordered one last round of drinks and turned to Tim.

"Tim, how about the Accounting Department? Have you got anything you can share with us?"

Tim looked around the table and hesitated. Finally, he said, "I-I, um, I'm impressed with what all you folks are doing. I don't really have anything, but we're working hard to, um, make sure that our books are in good order when the first half of the year is over. For the banks, I mean. I, uh, I can't really be creative with accounting processes like you all are doing. Accounting is accounting. There are rules, so all I can do is make sure all our numbers are good."

Andrea let him off the hook. "Tim's right. He's in a different situation than we are. We can easily change procedures, but accounting practices are pretty well set in stone. Just making sure the numbers are right is a big deal, though."

Everyone agreed and made some similar positive comments.

Robbie looked to Andrea and said, "We haven't heard from you yet, Andi."

"Well, I'm mostly focusing now on doing all we can to make certain we have an absolutely awesome production level in June. It wouldn't look good if we dropped the ball in the last month before the meeting."

As everyone agreed with that, Andrea continued, "But tomorrow night's meeting of the BizEd class should be very interesting. While I was trying to figure out what the subject matter would be, three of the Line 4 workers came up to talk to me. Turns out, they have some very interesting ideas about new products and changes to existing products that we could make that would cause us to stand out more from the competition. I'm telling you, I forced them to tell me a few of the ideas and they are absolutely dynamite. Gretch, if you can get the sales reps to sit in, I'd love to hear their reaction to some of these. In fact, I can hardly wait."

That set off another flurry of words bouncing back and forth as Tim watched on the sidelines. Finally, he looked at Andrea and asked, "So you're really going to keep having these business education meetings with the employees every week?"

"Yeah, we are," Andrea said, grinning widely. "They're fun. You should come down and participate. In fact, you should teach a session. Maybe explaining how the bank views a company balance sheet or something."

Starting his protest, Tim replied, Oh, I don't think—"

The others cut him off.

"Oh, yeah, that'd be good," Sammi said.

"Gotta do it, Tim. You'll see, it's fun," Robbie added.

The meeting went on for another fifteen minutes, and on a few occasions, Andrea thought she even saw Tim smile.

Andrea paid the tab and they called it a night. She left her car in the Juggernaut parking lot and Robbie gave her a lift home. He promised to come by and pick her up at 7:30.

Feeling quite good about how the meeting wrapped up, she bid Robbie a good night and headed to the apartment building door. One of the porch lights was burned out, and there were safer-looking places in town. She turned her key and looked back. Robbie was still parked there, watching for her safe entry intently, and she realized she didn't mind a bit.

WEDNESDAY, JUNE 6

Tim walked down the hall and joined Craig in his office on Wednesday morning.

Way past any pretense of niceties, Craig said, "What'd you find out?"

Tim pursed his lips a bit and said, "You shoulda been there. I don't know how you talked me into it. It was very uncomfortable."

"Why? Were they cold to you?"

Tim shook his head. "No. No, not really. But they are all good friends and they're working together in ways I've never seen here before."

"Like what?" Craig asked, as a hard rain hammered his windows on the south side of the building.

"Jeez, they've got all kinds of things going. They're moving fast. HR is making movies to help training and recruiting. Sales is organizing a Rapid Response Team for foul-ups and committees of workers to monitor marketplace changes. Shipping is creating new shifts to give them better coverage and get more product out. And Andrea is committed to this BizEd thing."

"So what's your read on it?" Craig asked, a bit worried that he didn't really want to know.

Tim shook his head. "Like I said, it made me uncomfortable. They're working hard to make sure the bank is impressed and doesn't turn us down. It feels a bit weird to, you know, be rooting against them."

"Doesn't matter," Craig said. "Our plan is still solid. Hell, long-term this company won't last anyway. We're just going to get ourselves in position to gently end it on our own terms. Do as we agreed. Doctor those books up so they don't reflect anything too good. Write off every bit of late or bad debt we can justify, and in another month, we'll be calling the shots. Stick with me, Tim. We're almost to the finish line."

WEDNESDAY, JUNE 13

A torrential downpour caused some flooding in various part of the city on June 6th. Many employees, worried about their kids getting home from school and rain damage to their homes, left right after work and the BizEd meeting was rescheduled for the 13th.

This time over seventy employees in the company were in attendance, including eleven from shipping, six from marketing and HR, the two accounting assistants, and a much stronger showing from manufacturing. After ordering a record number of sandwiches from the sub shop, Andrea double-checked her meals and entertainment budget and announced that the BizEd meeting would become an every-other-Wednesday event. As popular as it was, there was collective agreement that the new schedule was fine.

The meeting flew by in no time at all. Everyone was overwhelmed by the flood of creative ideas that the crew offered.

Of particular interest were ideas about adding a camera to the large outdoor Glimmer Stone Vases. The thought was that it could be aimed at the door and transmitted to the owner's phone so any activity would trigger it and allow the homeowner to see who was on their doorstep. All the technology exists already, and many were enthusiastic about the idea. Several employees suggested building in two-way communication and other features.

Others suggested new unique design contests for the customers; new shapes for the vases; totally different lines of products;

online interfaces that allowed customers to design their own decorative Glimmer Stone patterns; and much more. When it became time to stop and eat, people wanted more time to explain still more ideas. Finally, at 6:30, Andrea announced that it was time to eat and they would resume the next meeting on June 27th with a continuation of the same topic. That satisfied everyone, and the catered food was consumed easily in minutes.

As the evening came to a close, Andrea spotted Craig and Tim standing on the mezzanine level, watching the meeting unfold.

FRIDAY, JUNE 29

The team had blown past four thousand units produced by 3:45 yesterday afternoon. Seeing the unit count rise minute by minute, the lines worked at top speed and closed out the month with an all-time record of 4,291 completed units.

Morale was sky high as they finished off another successful month and made their largest bonus ever. In addition, scheduled long before anyone knew they would top the record today, all employees were looking forward to being served a fine catered meal. Andrea, Robbie, Gretchen, and Sammi had each kicked in a thousand dollars and convinced Bentley to have the company add another two thousand to celebrate in fashion. A fine Italian restaurant provided catering service at a modestly discounted rate for the hundred and twenty-six employees. Andrea had recruited her uncle to provide the liquid refreshments, and dinner was scheduled to begin at six o'clock.

Andrea smiled to herself as she remembered the meeting she'd had with the other three VPs and her supervisors when she first broached the subject.

She had finished explaining what they were going to do and they'd all agreed to the financing plan. Then she dropped the bombshell.

"So there's a method to my madness here. This dinner cele-bration is for the rank and file. All the employees of the different divisions. It's not for us."

Reading the look of confusion on their faces, Andrea quickly added, "Oh, yes, we'll get some food too, but the real purpose of this event is to thank the workers and to be the servant. Have you heard that phrase before?"

No one nodded or raised their hand.

"Being the servant is one of the seven keys to superior man-agement. On the 29th, we're taking it to the next level, and we will be the kitchen help, and the waiters, and the drink pourers while we wait on our employees' every need.

"We will practice servant leadership in the extreme. We do much of it now when we roll our sleeves up and jump into the fray—helping on the lines, building crates, making the sales calls ourselves, staying late to interview so you can fill a spot quickly. All of us are doing it, but what we need to do is make sure every employee recognizes it for what it is—our desire to serve them and provide them with what they need in order to do their jobs better.

"When we stop acting like the boss and start acting like a helper, then I think they get it more. No one is more important than the mission. Our personal needs do not come before the com-pany's or the employees'. And when we subjugate ourselves to them and to the bigger picture, that 'be the servant' attitude will instill your voice with authority that truly resonates."

She paused and looked around the room. "Does that make sense to everybody?"

Malik raised his hand and started speaking. "Andrea, I sort of get what you're talking about, but you almost make it sound like we work for them—for the employees."

"I know. It takes a little mind shift to grasp this. Look at it this way. If one of the employees came to you and said, 'Malik, we really each need a La-Z-Boy recliner to relax in during our breaks,' what would you say?"

Malik laughed and said, "Yeah, and I need a Maserati to drive to work every morning."

Everyone laughed. Andrea did too, then said, "Of course you would. We're not running a resort here. Just because they want something doesn't mean we'll jump and do it. But suppose that same person came to you and said, 'Malik, if we had a cold-water dispenser right here near the front of the lines, workers wouldn't have to be gone so long, going all the way into the Executive Offices to get a cup of water. Then we could all work faster and not have so much lost time.' So, Malik, what would you say to that?"

Malik nodded. "I get it. And it's a damn good idea, by the way. Then they'd be asking for something that makes sense."

"Right," Andrea agreed. "Our job is to be the facilitators. We need to give them the proper tools to do their job. If we save money by not providing the right tools, we just pay it out anyway in decreased productivity. And then there's the corollary to that," she added.

"What's that, Professor?" Sammi said, cackling her signature laugh.

"My uncle is the professor, but he's taught me all this stuff. The corollary is that as we give them the tools they need to do their job, the next step is to empower them to do more themselves. We've got smart, talented people here. We need to trust them more, and delegate more, and empower them to attack issues on their own. That's kinda scary sometimes, but when we release power to the employees, it's like magic. Amazing things happen, and, paradoxically, the act of releasing power actually increases your own."

Andrea remembered that the group bounced ideas around for another forty minutes before the meeting wrapped up. Now she stood on the stairway watching the caterers, managers, and supervisors preparing the makeshift dining area and mingling with the employees.

Under her breath, talking to herself, she mumbled, "I better roll up my sleeves and get down there before I fail to practice what I preach."

The dinner was a huge success. Smiles were everywhere as conversation flowed in every direction. The food was hot and excellent and—with the exception of Craig and Tim, who both begged off—management was doing a fine job of being the servant.

Arthur Bentley had joined them, taking a seat at the head of one of the tables and conversing more in one hour with the rank and file employees than he had in the last ten years combined.

Andrea made a point of thanking Mr. Bentley for bearing the bulk of the costs and praising his generosity to anyone who would listen. As the dinner wound down, she and her assistants delivered a fine tiramisu as dessert to everyone who was seated. She ate hers on the fly. As the noise volume slowly decreased, Andrea went to an open area up front and seized the microphone.

"I have just a few words to wrap up this celebration tonight. First of all, I want to thank Mr. Bentley again for making this evening possible. And I want to thank Robbie, Gretchen, and Sammi for contributing some funds to help pay for all the expenses. And not—"

"Hey, girl, you forgot to add yourself to that list," Sammi called out.

Andrea nodded. "I think we all did our part. I also have to thank tonight's servers—the VPs and Malik, Reese, and Meghan, who worked tirelessly to bring you drink refills and anything else your hearts desired."

They got a good-natured round of applause. Reese yelled out to everyone, "Don't forget to leave a huge tip!"

More laughter.

Andrea got right back to it. "Today we finished the month and the half year by breaking every record in the books with our 4,291st unit completed in one month. Ladies and gentlemen, all of you are incredible!"

Everyone stood and gave themselves a round of applause.

Certain she was finally done with the mandatory thank-yous, Andrea began the closing, which was really her purpose all along.

"I want you to think about what you've done in the last six months, and you should feel very proud. We've gone through a lot of changes together and I believe we've emerged on the other side with a greater appreciation for each other and for what we are achieving here.

"This world is changing so fast, we have to try new things, we have to take some risks, we have to be OK with the idea of failing occasionally so that we can succeed far more often. Juggernaut makes a high-quality product that not only *we* are proud of, but our customers are also proud to own them. We make lives better in small ways that add up to a much bigger outcome. Our products make the buyers happier and more content with what they own, because each and every one of you puts your all into making the finished product. I want to thank each one of you and tell you that together we can achieve great things. Like a hard-rowing boat crew, we can do more when we pull together than when we row by ourselves. And each of you is proving that over and over again, every day of the week. Thank you all for, well, just being brave enough to face change and deal with it."

And now for a brief intermission before we rejoin our story…

SUMMARY

The story you just read was, of course, a business book written as a novel. I did that for two major reasons. First of all, too many business books are sterile, dull, and uninspiring. Real life is messy and marginally more exciting, and now and then it can be inspiring. Secondly, in dealing with the pace of change, the most important ingredient is human nature. I wanted the reader to hear every conversation, to feel the fear and the angst that real people do when confronted with radical change. In business, nothing great can be achieved, or changed, without skillfully working with and through others.

I tried to entertain you and make you care a bit about Andrea and Tyler and all the others at Juggernaut Enterprises. I think we all learn better when we immerse ourselves in the characters and their world, so I added the requisite bad guys, competing interests, and a short-term deadline to increase the pace of the book and show you what could be done even in severely dire circumstances. So, if you found yourself caring about the characters, then that's a good sign. Why? Because if you are truly going to make a difference in the business world, you need to care fiercely, intensely, unendingly about the people your changes will impact.

Tyler and many others have said, "Nothing happens until someone sells something." I say nothing happens until someone buys something. There is no sale without the purchase, and for any manager to address significant change, someone, preferably everyone, has to *buy* in. The employees have to buy in. *Accepting* change isn't enough. They have to *embrace* it.

In Andrea's story, she finds herself in charge of the largest and most important department at Juggernaut. She recognizes that, more than anyone, she has to create significant change, and she begins with the employees and focuses on productivity because of the looming threat from the bank. What I want to be sure I communicate clearly here is the following:

> **Dealing with the pace of change is not the same as dealing with the pace of work.**

It is often interrelated and may be the focal point for all the changes planned, but it is not the end product or the only goal. In order to deal with the ever-increasing pace of change, you need a *team of people* who trust each other, work together, and row their boat in the same direction. You need a team that is dedicated to doing whatever it takes, to making any change necessary to get their boat across the finish line first. That requires stalwart dedication to the process of change. Your goal is not to necessarily increase the speed with which you perform, but to create the processes and mechanisms to sustain the change.

> **Create systems that self-perpetuate and put them on autopilot so they inherently sustain themselves.**

Let's look at what Andrea did.

Skipping over the pity-party portion and her own fears and misgivings that any normal person would experience in a similar position, Andrea took the first step toward a quality response.

She went to see her mentor. She had to move quickly, but she needed focus, too. In normal circumstances (without a fabricated bank deadline), business owners and managers could move more slowly and carefully. They could hold meetings, solicit input, form committees, and work harder to gain consensus on what should be done. Abe Lincoln said, "If I had eight hours to chop down a tree, I'd spend six sharpening my axe." Andrea didn't have that opportunity, so she went to Tyler and talked it all out. Fortunately, Tyler told her the truth: she couldn't do it alone and her first objective had to be winning the hearts and minds of the employees.

> **Communication, employee growth, reinforcement —all must come before trust is built.**

Again, in this severe example, Andrea didn't have the luxury of time to build support beforehand, so she moved to the next step before trust was built. Certainly a gamble, but the time constraints in the story gave her no other option. Her next step was to create incentive, to give the employees a personal reason to participate.

Andrea designed a bonus program. She made some mistakes in selecting the goals, but she was smart enough to forewarn everyone that making the perfect bonus plan on the first try was exceedingly difficult. Admitting that upfront took away some of the sting of being wrong. As humbling as it was for her to admit her error, she scored more points by changing the goal in the employee's favor and looking human in the process.

In the real world, many managers have created bonus plans that failed miserably. As a result, they generally don't try again and they form the opinion that bonus plans always fail. But bonus plans, in general, don't fail because they are inherently flawed. They fail because they weren't designed properly. Andrea read books on the structure of proper bonus plans and she knew what she had to do.

Next, Andrea restructured the review and raise process. She saw firsthand how unhealthy the once-a-year, fixed interval review process was and how it could be improved through delinking. At the end of this book, I list some resources you can access for more information on the delinking process, bonus plan construction, and people management. If you want more details, have a good read.

After Andrea started up the new "anytime" raise program, she spent time training the front-line supervisors and teaching them exactly how to make the raise decisions and how to handle the conversations. Training the front-line supervisors is critical to success. Those supervisors need to be trusted as well. Andrea made sure that they wasted no time handing out the raises that were deserved. That was critical!

She followed that up with plenty of reinforcement. People need to know how they are doing. Good reinforcement is personalized when possible (e.g., the individualized weekly reports showing each person's forecasted bonus amount). She also created visual events to accent it (giving out the jackets, installing the scoreboard). Teaching the supervisors about 'catching someone doing something right' and being the servant (at the dinner party) were important steps to gaining trust.

Andrea added a weekly meeting for training and education for the employees. This is the enlightenment part. Smarter, more informed employees are an *asset*, not a danger. Let them understand what is going on, why certain decisions are made. Strive for transparency. Share the numbers and equations with them. Help them become better business people. When they understand, for example, why labor cost has to be controlled and managed, they will be more able to work within the system to align their personal goals with the company goals. Ultimately, that is what you need to do to build a nimble workforce that embraces change instead of fighting it.

A few other things Andrea did that are necessary to stay on top of the pace of change: She recruited her counterparts in the other departments to work with her. She held out an olive branch or two to Mr. Bentley, preserving her options with regard to working with him. She grasped the urgency of the situation and pushed everything to happen faster.

After reading the story and sort of living it yourself, I trust you can see how difficult it would be to turn a company in a different direction quickly in order to survive changing markets, competition, and general societal values. Research has shown that somewhere between 50 and 75 percent of corporate change efforts fail. What's more, the usual timetable for a corporate transformation is three to five years. That's a long time to spend on an effort that fails. Doing it the right way is simply not a solitary job. Keeping pace with change demands teamwork throughout the company and continuity of purpose.

Andrea realized fairly early on that her department was impacted heavily by the performance of the others. If shipping was not able to keep up, they couldn't count on getting everything out the door to the customer on time. If sales were not performing, they couldn't count on a steady volume of work. If HR was sleeping on the job, they wouldn't have quality applicants for future growth. Major change requires that all the departments are working in concert with each other.

Lastly, you may have read about some companies successfully reinventing themselves and coping with changing and difficult circumstances. Delving deeper, I think you'd also find that one leader was so strong and charismatic that the force of his or her will achieved the change. And after that leader passed from the scene, the company's success didn't always continue. Most business owners or managers are not Steve Jobs or Oprah Winfrey. Most of us are just people who care about other people and want to do the right thing.

So, if you aren't necessarily a famous, high-profile, charismatic leader, how do you force long-lasting change?

You build systems.

In most cases, those who make the business alterations necessary to cope with the pace of change have to look at the long-range picture. They have to design systems that are self-perpetuating so when the architect is no longer around, they continue to do their job.

Self-perpetuating systems are those that inherently provide for cycles of repeating events: alignment of goals, incentives, constant reinforcement, and appropriate rewards. These repeating cycles act to increase employee confidence that helping the company reach its targets will serve to help them achieve their individual goals as well.

What you are seeking to do is to continually align the employees' **enlightened self-interest** with the company goals. Goals will change and bonus programs, raises, review processes, hiring, disciplining, and every aspect of business will change over time, but the Cycles of Repeating Events must remain the same.

ALIGN * INCENTIVIZE * REINFORCE * REWARD

Align the employee's enlightened self-interest with the corporate goals of the times. Create self-perpetuating incentive programs (those that work whether a leader or champion is pushing them or not). You can do that by integrating consistent on-going bonus programs into the compensation package. Don't think of monthly bonus payments as something temporary; think of it as a normal component of the pay package. Next, continue to reinforce performance and then consistently reward appropriately. When you do that, the company becomes more nimble and flexible and the resistance to change is far lower when the employees believe in both management *and* the corporate culture, which is based on the Cycle of Repeating Events.

For all future growth, you need a nimble and flexible workforce that embraces the changes to be made but has the confidence that the corporate culture will always remain the same.

For example, if demand for a key product line dissipates, your company must be able—and willing—to adapt for the good of the company *and* the employees. Together, the management and the employees can attack the problem, identify solutions, make changes, and adjust their goals. That requires the company leadership to embrace employee participation and utilize a heavy degree of decentralization so changes can be made faster and still integrate effectively with the overall corporation. That can be done when the employees have the confidence that although details may change, the commitment to the Cycle of Repeating Events will not waver.

In summary, one leader, like Andrea, can create the proper atmosphere for this kind of success, but it takes a continuing corporate culture to ensure it endures. That can only happen when everyone is in the same boat, rowing in the same direction.

Now back to the story…

THURSDAY, JULY 5

Tim left the Accounting Department that morning at 9:15 and strolled down the hall to Craig's corner office. Craig's secretary looked up from her work and signaled that he could go on in.

Dispensing with any small talk, Craig immediately asked, "The finance report done?"

"I got your copy here," Tim said as he handed it over.

Fidgeting in his chair already, Tim added, "It's the best I could do."

"Shit, Tim, this shows a profit for June," Craig said.

"Yeah, but we lost a little bit for the quarter," Tim replied defensively.

"I thought you were gonna doctor these up a bit." Craig stood up and walked to the window. Continuing, he asked, "What happened to those tricks you had? What about the bad debt?"

"Craig, I wrote off a ton in April. I knew a bunch weren't really bad debt, they were just slow payers. So they paid in May and June. Those payments then were a credit to bad debt, and I didn't have enough debits to wipe them out. As it is, these bad debts I claimed at the end of June are bogus too. There's only so much I can do without the bank figuring it out. I mean, it all has to balance."

"Did you put in the bonuses I suggested for all of our staff?" Craig asked.

"They're in there. That adds another eight thousand in cost and pushed the quarterly losses up higher, but it wasn't enough to really impact June," Tim replied.

"OK, OK, I know," Craig said, rubbing his chin. "OK, this is what we'll do. Don't show Bentley the June P&L. That damn woman cranked out so many units, she undid everything we've been working on. We'll just show him the quarterly report with the loss."

Tim shook his head. "We can't lie to him, Craig. We have to—"

Cutting the CFO off, Craig blurted, "This is no time to get cold feet. Just follow my lead. We'll present an ugly picture and convince Bentley to accept our offer."

"I don't see—"

"Tim, just follow my lead and quit your worrying. This will work. Come on, let's go now."

Craig didn't wait for an answer. He stormed out of his office and headed down the hall toward Bentley's suite.

By 10:30, Craig and Tim had gone over the P&L and balance sheet with the Chairman of the Board and painted the bleakest picture possible for the company.

"I don't know," Bentley said, hesitating. "I think that the employees were really starting to like me. Andrea has them working hard, and I thought we turned the corner—"

"Arthur," Craig said, using his given name as if they were close friends. "I know there's been some positive things happening and people are in a better state of mind now, but it's not reflected in the financials. We lost money for the second quarter in a row. Her bonuses and frequent raises are killing us. We have to face facts."

Arthur Bentley stared at Craig, then turned to Tim. "You think if I step down and you take over and cut out all these extra costs, the bank will loan us the money one more time?"

Employing all his acting skills, Craig whispered his response. "It's the only chance we have. Using backchannels, I already told the bank that we know that the bonuses and all the other changes that Andrea made look good but have set us back, not forward. I told them we would let her go, reverse those programs, and start working for a profit again."

"Maybe I should stay and fire her myself and you could take over her position and—"

Cutting off his boss again, Craig shook his head and said, "I suggested that, and the bank already nixed it. They said that ship had sailed. You had your chance to fire her and you didn't follow through, and now they only trust me to do it."

Bentley slumped in his chair. He put his hand to his chin and sat there like a stone statue for several minutes. Finally, in a slow parade of despairing words, he said, "So how do we do this?"

Tim let out a sigh of relief, earning him a death stare from Craig. "Arthur, you're still the company owner and now you're just elevated to Chairman Emeritus. I'll take on all the responsibility of President and Chairman, and you don't have to do that anymore. As we showed you, I'll cut costs, and we'll be able to pay you fifteen percent more than your current salary and you'll still get dividends later down the road. It's the best deal we can do."

Bentley just nodded.

Craig rose from his seat, tapped Tim on the shoulder to do likewise, and headed for the door. "Bankers will be here at three. We'll make our best presentation then."

Again Bentley nodded and looked down into his lap.

Craig grinned all the way down the hall.

At 2:45, all the VPs and Bentley met in the board room, and immediately Craig took control of the meeting. "The bankers called and said they were running a little late and would be here by 3:15. We sent them the latest financials, which show us losing one point eight percent in the second quarter."

"Losing nearly two percent?" Robbie asked. "I thought we were doing pretty good."

"Costs rose, we had some bad debt, payroll increased, and we had a huge severance payment to Charlie because of his firing. It would have been far better to keep him on, but I don't run Manufacturing, so I can't help what happened there," Craig replied.

Andrea stared at him, but before she could formulate a response, Gretchen asked, "So what are you saying? That after all this effort to change things up, the bank's just going to give us a big fat *no*?"

Tim spoke up. "Well, I think—"

"I just brought on the best sales rep we've ever had," Gretchen shouted. "My new commission structure is really working great. We've got a ton of new orders coming in. They can't pull the plug now!"

Seconds later, Sammi and Gretchen were quizzing both Craig and Tim on how the financials could fail to show the improved sales.

"Sammi!" Tim yelled. "Pipe down. You don't even know what you're talking about. The new orders your guys brought in haven't even been processed yet. We can't declare the sales until the items are manufactured and shipped. That was our deal with the bank."

"Wait!" Bentley called out. "This is the first I heard of a ton of new sales. Can't we show that to the bank and maybe I can stay and—"

"Listen, everybody!" Craig said, trying to restore order and quiet Bentley before he said one thing too much. "We've been through this. The bank has rules, and they said they would make their decision based on the end of the second quarter financials. It is what it is and—"

Craig ceased talking as the trio of bankers arrived at the door to the conference room.

Changing his tone instantly, he said, "Gentlemen, please come in, and we have three seats here on the right set out for you. Would any of you want some coffee?"

They each declined and sat down at the table. The one in the center introduced each of them, but Andrea's mind was a blur, struggling to understand what was really going on. Craig quickly introduced the other VPs. The bankers all wore different colored ties, so she assigned them names in her mind—Mr. Blue Tie, Mr. Green Tie, and Mr. Red Tie.

The leader of the three, Mr. Green Tie, began the conversation.

"We've had several informal conversations with Mr. Saunders and Mr. Russell about the financials, and we had time to look them over earlier today. We've also talked with some employees as we did our due diligence, and frankly, those conversations have not been very favorable toward management."

"Who did you talk to?" Andrea asked.

Blue Tie looked through a pile of papers, checking his notes. Before Green Tie could shut him up, he said, "A fellow named Charlie Jensen contacted us and told us about some issues he was concerned about, and we also talked with a line worker, Ricky Stamper, who—"

Green Tie interrupted his associate. "It's probably not appropriate to discuss specific names, Jim. Ladies and gentlemen, the fact is that during our analysis of your company, we learned a lot. We understand you have made several failed attempts to gain greater productivity out of the Manufacturing Department and that has resulted—"

"Excuse me!" Andrea interrupted. "*Failed* attempts?"

Clearing his throat, Green Tie said, "I'm sorry, perhaps failed is a slightly harsh word, but it's clear that the numbers do not—"

"You want to see some numbers?" Andrea asked. "You come with me and I'll show you some numbers. Have you once stepped foot onto our manufacturing floor?"

Stuttering now, Green Tie mumbled, "Well, we normally, um…"

Rising quickly from her seat, Andrea motioned everyone to follow. "It's this way to manufacturing," she called out loudly to get their attention and to drown out whatever Craig was trying to say.

She led the trio of bankers and all the rest of those in the boardroom down from the mezzanine level to the manufacturing floor. There, she let them feast their eyes on what she had created.

"These are the six lines of the manufacturing process," Andrea said, speaking loudly to be heard over the din. "Up there is the new scoreboard we installed to give us up-to-date data on how much of each product we are making today and how that affects our statistics for both productivity and the bonus program. In a minute the scoreboard will quit displaying the basic numbers and will show more detail."

Andrea paused and then yelled out to Sue on Line 1, "Sue, is that Malik sleeping again in his office?"

The bankers' eyes grew wide.

"No, ma'am! He's doing some coaching with Mandy. You want me to get that slacker out here for you?"

"Sure," Andrea said, smiling.

A few moments later, the six-foot-five Malik stepped out of his office with a bewildered look on his face.

Andrea motioned him over, calling Reese and Meghan over too.

Looking at the bankers, she said, "This is Malik; he is the supervisor for Lines 1 and 2. Reese does 3 and 4, while Meghan handles 5 and 6. How are we doing today, guys?'

Meghan jumped in. "We're doing great! These guys hardly need us anymore. We're on a brisk pace today, and there's been a lot of cheering going on."

Red Tie stepped closer and asked, "Cheering?"

"Whenever the team hits a milestone number of units made," Reese explained, "Thomas over there, the big guy, he bellows out the number and everyone knows they just made a little bit more bonus. In fact, you can see on the scoreboard, we are sitting at 209 units so far today. In a moment…wait, here it comes…"

Thomas tagged the item at the end of Line 6, tapped something into his computer keypad, and yelled out "Two hundred and ten!"

The floor erupted into cheers.

Andrea checked her watch and smiled. "Three thirty-five and already at 210? You guys are really humming!"

Watching with great interest, the bankers looked around at the sea of smiling faces. Red Tie asked, "Do they, um, do they all know why we're here?"

"They haven't got the faintest idea. They don't even know who you are," Andrea replied. "This is what we do every day. And at the pace they are going now, today will be the second or third most productive day we've ever had. This, gentlemen, is productivity. And it hasn't failed."

Just then, Malik walked over to Line 2 and called out, "You heard Thomas. 210? Is that all? My grandmother could do five hundred in a day all by herself. I think maybe you guys are the slackers."

A chorus of "No! You are!" came from the members of the line, followed by a cascade of laughter.

Andrea moved closer to the bankers and said, "Malik's no slacker and they know it. He works harder than all of them. They love him so they give him a hard time. That's what we do here."

Blue Tie looked up at the scoreboard and said, "It shows $804 in the bonus pool. What does that mean?"

"Every unit they complete adds a certain number of dollars to the pool. At the end of the month, that money is distributed to everyone on a prorated basis per hour worked," Andrea explained.

"How much did they get last month?" he asked.

"Last month, the total bonus was $56,922. The average worker got a bonus for the month of a little more than $600."

"That's too much! That's why you're losing money," he replied, then turned to Green Tie, smiling broadly, as though he had just broken the code on the Rosetta Stone.

Andrea motioned with her arm again to have them follow her. She escorted the bankers to the Shipping Department, where she pushed Robbie in front of the trio and let him explain all the changes he had made.

When Robbie was done, Andrea led them to the Human Resources office, where Sammi proudly showed them the new meet-and-greet process and displayed some of the training videos they had made.

That was followed with a visit to Sales, where Gretchen explained her new commission structure and how it was resulting in far better sales, even though they didn't show up yet on the financials. She introduced her new star salesperson and, assuming these men were potential buyers, the rep raved about the product quality and the work ethic all throughout the building. After ten minutes, Gretchen pried him away, whispering in his ear that they were bankers, not buyers.

Andrea wasn't done. She looked at Tim and said, "Tim, let's show them your office and team next, and you can tell them all about the changes that you've made." She smiled at him, mercilessly, knowing he had nothing to show.

Checking his watch and making a big fuss out of it, Craig rescued his buddy and said, "We really haven't got time for more show and tell. Let's return to the boardroom where it is quieter and we can discuss a few more details."

Craig shot a glance at Andrea, transmitting a message of "enough already" that Andi had no trouble interpreting. She smiled back at him.

Returning to the boardroom, Craig immediately took charge and did his best to control the conversation. Green Tie sat down and said, "That was all very interesting. I appreciate the tour, Andrea."

Craig took center stage again. "Fact is, Mr. Davis," he said, looking at Green Tie, "we have been trying very hard to do some things differently, and some have worked well and others not so well." He purposely glanced in Andrea's direction as he finished the last remark.

"After a lot of discussion, Arthur has agreed to be elevated to Chairman Emeritus and I will take over as President and Chairman. As I told you before, I will restore the previous policies regarding reviews and raises and the failed bonus program experiment. That will cut costs and bring us back to profitability. We will—"

"Excuse me, Craig," Green Tie interrupted. "Before we get too far along here, I would like to say that Arthur Bentley has been a great client of the bank for a long time and we value our relationship with him. Arthur, I want to tell you how impressed I am with your company morale and the willingness you have shown to experiment and try new things. I think that speaks well of you, and I applaud your decision to let the others take over."

Turning away from Arthur toward the new President, Green Tie continued, "But, Craig, I'm confused about this bonus program, and I'm wondering if you might be on to something. The crew certainly seemed stoked. Could you tell me how you all came up with it and what the theory is behind it?"

"Um, well, I…believe me, I can understand why you're confused. It's…well, it's a bit hard to explain."

Andrea stood up and said, "No, it's not. I'm happy to explain it. And I'll tell you why paying out $56,000 is not too much of a bonus. In fact, I'll tell you why it would be better for us if it were a lot higher."

Intrigued even more now, Green Tie opened his mouth to speak, but was cut off.

"Now, wait a minute," Craig butted in. "She's the one who convinced Bentley to go forward with her plan. I've tried to protect her here, but what you'll be hearing is just a bunch of sales pitch nonsense. The bonus amounts are too high and that is what has caused us to have a losing quarter. I don't think anyone can argue with that."

"I can," claimed Andrea.

"I'd like to hear it," Green Tie said.

Andrea walked to the head of the table and stood next to Bentley. She put her left hand on his shoulder and said, "This man—this man is *something*. He argued with me, quite persuasively, that I should not restructure the employee compensation so radically. But after a long discussion, he agreed that if ever there was a time to make radical change, this was it. That took nerve, and I have been doing all I can to keep from letting him down."

Andrea paused for a moment, trying to resist the urge to blush over all those creative embellishments on the truth.

"First of all, I met with all the workers and told them that our competition was gaining ground and if we didn't do something unique and different, there would be bad times ahead. Then I cut everyone's pay by ten percent."

She stared at the bankers and got the desired response of surprise and horror that she hoped for.

"Oh, did Craig forget to tell you that? Cutting their pay by ten percent lopped off about three hundred dollars per worker from their monthly salaries. Then I instituted a bonus plan that, upon performing the same as they had for years, they would get a bonus roughly equal to the amount that they lost. But, if they had a bad month—and we've had a few in our day—they would make less than before. And if they had a good month, producing more units than usual, they would get a share of the profits from those extra units via the bonus payment, earning extra pay."

"So, sorry, I'm still not following it all," Blue Tie declared. "Why did you cut their pay if they were just going to earn it back via normal production?"

"What I was doing," Andrea replied, "was changing the *reason* we pay people. Before the bonus program started, we essentially paid everyone in manufacturing for *showing up*. That's it. All they had to do was clock in and we paid them. So if they felt like working slowly and the number of units produced was low, it didn't matter. They got their pay anyway."

Andrea slowed down and took a breath, then continued, "With the new pay structure, we now pay them something for showing up and any other pay above and beyond that is paid for their performance. That changes all the dynamics because, essentially, that last ten percent was the difference between a good day and a poor day. Now they're motivated to maintain a minimum acceptable level of production in order to keep their pay level the same as before."

Red Tie scratched his head and said, "OK, I'm getting that now, but what about what you said earlier: why would it be better if the bonus amounts were higher? That doesn't make any sense."

Andrea smiled back at Red Tie. "The bonus is structured to motivate them to do more, to work faster and harder all day long. The amount that we put in the bonus pool for each extra unit completed is only a small fraction of the average product profit. In other words, since labor cost is not any higher than it always was, the bonus is the only extra cost associated with each unit created. Juggernaut makes more money on every extra unit made. The employees make more, too. And lastly, the customer now is more likely to get their item shipped a day or two sooner than we used to, so they also win. Everybody wins. Even the bank, because now we are producing more at lower cost and earning higher profits than ever."

The trio exchanged glances with each other.

Andrea poured it on. "You can do the math yourself. We don't count a sale until the item is completed and shipped. If you compute manufacturing labor cost as a percentage of revenues, you'll see that the higher the bonus paid, the lower the labor and the cost of goods is as a percentage. Makes paying the bank back even easier."

"And...and all this happened because of one change with the compensation structure?"

Andrea shook her head. "No, that's not true. We did a combination of many things. For example, we drastically revamped our review and raise process to increase employee motivation."

"How did you do that?" Blue Tie asked.

"We delinked reviews and raises. That is, we quit giving one formal review a year and following it up with a yearly raise. Now, we give frequent and multiple coaching sessions where we explain what the employee has to improve on in order to get his or her next raise. Then we grant raises—small, average, big, whatever—as we see the improvement happening. We now allow employees to get multiple raises in a short period of time. So instead of them hoping to get one raise a year and then kicking back a bit and bringing their game up again just before next year's raise time, we've shown them that they could get a raise *any* day."

"So you're paying them even more than normal?" Red Tie asked.

"Some of them we are and some we're not. Depends on how hard they want to work," Andrea replied.

"That explains it!" Blue Tie asserted. "That's why the company didn't make a profit in the second quarter. You're giving out too many raises."

"No. If we were, labor costs as a percentage of sales would be rising. But they aren't. I did the math already. Labor cost has historically run at 28 percent of revenue. In April, it was 26 percent. May finished at 25.4 percent, and June dropped down to 24.7 percent of revenue."

"But you are paying more, right?" Blue Tie asked.

"Yes, we are," Andrea agreed. "Look, it's all relative. We're producing much more, too. What if you had two employees and one of them progressed at normal speed and got a normal raise in his first year and a normal raise in his second year, but the other employee worked faster and harder. Who would you value more? I mean, suppose the second employee progressed so quickly that he reached second-year performance levels after only one year. Doesn't he deserve more than the normal raise? I mean, how bad could that be? Now, after only one year, you have a rising star you can count on who shaved twelve months off the learning curve. Yes, you're paying more, but you're also getting back more."

Blue Tie mulled that over for a second.

Andrea followed up, "All we're doing is taking away barriers to employee growth. We're saying if you can improve significantly, we'll pay more than usual because now we have a more valuable asset in that worker. Why would you ever want to artificially limit people?"

Green Tie eyed her. "So you did those two things and suddenly everybody was onboard and you started seeing change right away?"

Andrea took a sip of her water and started in again. "Not at all. We suffered through some discontent and had our share of naysayers. Some of them tried to sabotage our efforts. It took a while. There were some rough days. Some people were moved or released. For example, I fired Charlie Jensen, the former Lines 3 and 4 Supervisor, because he only cared about one thing." She let that hang in the air for a few seconds.

As Red Tie was about to ask what that was, she said, "Charlie only cared about Charlie. I wanted him to care about his people, his crew. He was slowing me down, and in light of the bank's deadline for improvement, I didn't have any time to spare. So I replaced him with Reese Donnelley, because Reese actually gives a damn about his employees and about the company.

"What we've had to do here, gentlemen, to win the battle against our competitors and to keep up with the constant changes heading our way, is build a team. A team that will stand up to anything. A team that works hard for themselves and their company. A team that knows that the company cares back, and when you build that team, you make sure you align the employees' enlightened self-interest with the corporate goals, and that is what these changes I've described all do."

Andrea stopped to catch a breath and collect her thoughts.

Craig opened his mouth to say something, but Green Tie beat him to it. "Andrea, I sort of missed that last part. You said, 'Aligning the employee's'…um, what?"

Looking Green Tie straight in the eyes, she replied, "Napoleon said, 'Man is moved by two levers only—fear and self-interest.' We've been operating with fear. It doesn't work. After a period of time, fear loses its potency and dies a lonely death. Self-interest grows stronger and lives forever. When you create a system that pays the employee more to excel at what impacts the bottom line positively and educate him or her about business, then the enlightened employee works to serve his own self-interest and, by doing so, serves the company as well. All you have to do is get everyone into the same boat and show them how to row in the same direction—not because management wants them too, but because *they* want to, for themselves. And when you can do that, you've built a team that no competitor can top."

The room grew very quiet. Andrea pursed her lips slightly and took her seat again.

Craig immediately stood up and said, "You're not buying all that, are you?"

Green Tie stared back at him. "Excuse us while we step outside a moment and discuss what our decision will be." The trio left the room and walked ten feet down the hall until they were out of sight, stopping there to discuss what they'd learned.

Gretchen swallowed hard and everyone realized her gulp was the only sound they could hear in the room. They all sat there with their own silent thoughts torturing them with each second that passed.

Twelve minutes later, the bankers returned.

Still standing, Green Tie looked at Arthur Bentley and said, "Arthur, we'd like to hear your thoughts on this."

"What do you want to know?" Bentley asked.

"After all this was discussed, do you still want to be Chairman Emeritus?"

Bentley looked down at the floor. He started to speak, then held up. Finally, he said, "I never really wanted to resign. Craig sort of convinced me it was a good idea. This is my company, and I know I'm an old man and sometimes I don't understand the young people and the way that this world is changing, but I like that some of them do understand it better. I'd like to stay on as Chairman, but I've learned some things in the last six months and I found that I care, kind of like my father did, about the employees and what they think of working here. So, I think, if I stayed, I'd, well, I'd do a better job."

Green Tie nodded and asked, "Arthur, are you still fine with Craig as your President?"

Bentley hesitated, and as he did, Green Tie jumped in and said, "Or would you like to appoint someone else…perhaps Ms. Lane?"

"What!" Craig nearly exploded. "Are you serious? We had dinners and lunches together. You know me. You've never even met her before today."

Green Tie didn't respond. He just stared at Bentley. Finally he said, "Arthur? Do you have a thought on this?"

Arthur Bentley locked eyes with Green Tie and said, "I do. I think I'd choose to work with Ms. Lane."

Green Tie smiled and looked at his two associates. Then, smiling in Bentley's direction, he said, "Arthur, we decided to give you your loan, but at an increase of one point five percent on the interest rate for this round, if you selected Andrea as your President. If you selected Craig, we would've declined to make the loan. Would you care to make it official right now?"

As a flabbergasted Craig Saunders stared wide-eyed at the bankers, Red Tie pulled out a contract, entered Andrea's name in a blank line, and handed the contract to Bentley.

Bentley signed it immediately and said, "I hereby announce that Andrea Lane is the new President of Juggernaut Enterprises effective at this moment. Andrea, do you have any orders for us?"

Stunned, but still functioning, she said, "Yes, I have…I have three: Craig, your services are no longer needed. Don't let the door hit you in the ass on the way out. Tim, you can go with him or you can stay, but if you stay, you're doing things my way or you won't be staying long. Anyone staying, meet me at Brannigan's in fifteen minutes. I'm buying dinner, and I expect to hear a constant flow of new ideas for all the things we can improve on."

Craig pouted, screamed at Mr. Bentley, and stormed out. Andrea rose from her seat, and suddenly several hands were thrusted toward her for a congratulatory shake. The four other VPs shook her hand along with the three bankers. Bentley smiled broadly as he extended his hand as well.

Tim came over and said, "I've never seen anyone do what you've done. I'm sorry for my part in this. I'd like to stay."

Andrea looked him in the eyes and said, "Join us at Brannigan's tonight and you and I will talk about new ground rules tomorrow."

Tim nodded and put his hand out to her.

Andrea shook it, knowing she needed a knowledgeable CFO from the get-go.

As the meeting dissipated, Andrea walked down the hall to her office to pick up her coat and purse.

I'll call Uncle Tyler later tonight and tell him. He won't believe it—or maybe, maybe that sly fox will. I wonder if—

Her reverie was interrupted by Robbie knocking lightly on her door.

"Congratulations!" he said, smiling.

Turning quickly to him, she said, "Thanks. I…uh, I'm still a little stunned."

"I bet," Robbie said. "Look, I don't want to rain on your parade, but I have an opportunity I can't pass up, so I'll be handing in my one-month notice tomorrow."

"You're quitting?"

"I have to," Robbie said.

"Why? What are you gonna do?"

"I got pretty cozy with the owner of Top Delivery. He wants to retire and sell the business to someone who has more energy and will treat the employees right. I'd like to run my own show, and he's going to make me a good deal." Robbie looked down at the floor for a moment, then back up to Andrea.

Continuing, he added, "Besides, after seeing what you've done here, I've got all kinds of ideas about how to create a bonus program for their drivers—you know, rewarding on-time delivery and safe driving and stuff, and then delinking reviews and raises. And, you know, I think these are things that any kind of industry could use. And, hey, I'm on the board of the local Warehouse Manager Association and everybody knows me. I think I can get a lot more business and grow this puppy way up."

"Wow. So that's *the what* you're going to do. You didn't tell me *the why*," Andrea asked, eyeing him carefully.

"Well, hell, that should be obvious," Robbie replied. "It'd be kinda awkward, wouldn't it?"

"What do you mean?"

Robbie smiled and said, "I want to take our relationship to the next level. Well, I mean, if you do, too. I can't be seriously dating my own boss, can I?"

"Oh…oh! Oh, I…I fully agree. That would be so awkward for you. There you go, always thinking about yourself again." She leaned over and pecked him on the cheek.

"Come on, let's go," Andrea said. "Can't be late to the celebration party. We've still got a company to build."

THE END

* Author's note: OK, I admit it—I'm a sucker for a happy ending. *Your* results may vary. However, I guarantee that management's degree of satisfaction will depend on the level of trust you build with the employee base. Staying ahead of the pace of change is not a battle you can win by yourself. You need an enlightened self-interested team.

To succeed in today's fast-paced business world, your corporate culture needs to be based on a Cycle of Repeating Events that propels your team forward to overcome the pace of change.

RESOURCES

BONUS YOUR WAY TO PROFITS!

By Gary Brose

169 Pages

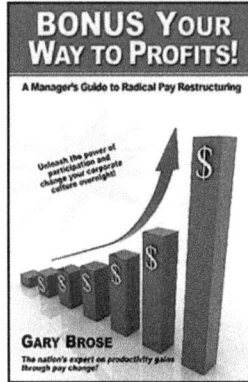

Price: Paperback $15.95 eBook $9.95

Change your Corporate Culture! Re-energize your company by restructuring your compensation package. Motivate your employees to care about the same things YOU do with a bonus program process that works EVERY time!

30 years of trial and error has produced a blueprint for increasing profits by "dangling the right carrot"!

Follow the guidelines proven in real life by business owner Gary Brose and you will be on the receiving end of a three-way win: for your employees, your customers, and YOU! This is not about giving away money or paying more. "Bonus Your Way to Profits!" shows the reader how to RESTRUCTURE pay to create a three-way win every time.

Read all about:

- The 8 Essential Elements
- Examples of bonus programs that succeeded and failed.
- Step-by-step design instructions
- Sample memos to your staff
- How to handle objections
- Transition Instructions

Buy on Amazon today: Order here

THE ULTIMATE MOTIVATED EMPLOYEE
By Gary Brose
Paperback, 142 Pages

Price: Paperback $14.95 eBook $7.99

Are your employees unmotivated and uninspired? Can you imagine how much better it would be if they were all on the same page as you are?

After 25 years of real-world trial and error, Gary Brose has identified the seven steps to a more productive workforce. Simple techniques business owners and managers can use to engage their employees and get them all pulling together.

This isn't a theory. These are proven methods Gary identified by comparing notes with other managers and through years of agonizing trial and error in the real world, in real time, with real flesh-and-blood employees! You will learn how to make several small changes in the way you interact with your workers that will get them to care as you do. You will see dozens of examples with real life stories from other business owners who understand the same principles.

Don't wait until it is too late. Start today with this easy-to-read, entertaining, and thought-provoking book about YOU and your management style!

Available on Amazon: Order here

Another book highly recommended:

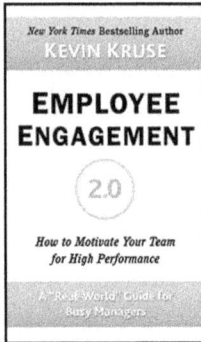

Imagine if you could:

EMPLOYEE
ENGAGEMENT
2.0

- Create massive emotional motivation and commitment among all your direct reports
- Turn apathetic groups into high performance teams exhibiting huge discretionary effort
- Be a leader who people fight to work with
- Win a "Best Place to Work" award within 12 months.

Indeed, you can do all that and more, and it doesn't take a lot of time or a big budget.

This isn't just another ivory tower book on leadership. Employee Engagement 2.0 is the result of both massive research and real-world experience. The author, Kevin Kruse, is a former Best Place to Work winner, serial entrepreneur, and NY Times bestselling author. He has advised dozens of organizations, from Fortune 500 companies, like SAP, to startups and non-profits and even to the US Marines.

This is your step-by-step guide that will teach you:

- What employee engagement is (it does not mean happy or satisfied)
- How engagement directly drives sales, profits, and even stock price
- The secret recipe for making anyone feel engaged
- How to quantify engagement, even if you have no budget
- 7 questions to ask that will identify your engagement weakness
- What to say to facilitate a team meeting on engagement
- A communication system that ensures rapid, two-way flow of information
- How to make your strategic vision memorable and "sticky"
- How to implement a complete engagement plan in only 8 weeks!

Being a great leader—one who drives massive passion, commitment, and engagement—is within your reach. Follow the step-by-step plan in Employee Engagement 2.0 and prepare to be a great place to work.

Buy Employee Engagement 2.0 today at https://amzn.to/2rBpyaF

Gary Brose is available to make appearances at your next corporate Event as a Keynote speaker, presenter or workshop leader. For current rates and more information, visit www.SmallBizSherpa.com

www.ingramcontent.com/pod-product-compliance
Lightning Source LLC
Chambersburg PA
CBHW021033210326
41598CB00016B/1001